THE FAMILY DOCTOR SPEAKS:

TURKEY TALES
&
BIBLE TRUTHS

ROBERT E. JACKSON JR., M.D.

ISBN 978-1-940645-80-3

COURIER PUBLISHING

Greenville, South Carolina
CourierPublishing.com

PRINTED IN THE UNITED STATES OF AMERICA

TABLE OF CONTENTS

Tom Turkey (Gene and Shannon Ridings, used by permission)

INTRODUCTION

TURKEY HUNTERS ANONYMOUS

Ten men sat in a circle in metal folding chairs in the basement of a downtown Methodist church. It was apparent they were uncomfortable and didn't want to be there. They gave furtive glances at one another and at the group leader. Mostly, they stared at their boots. They were all clothed in various amounts of camo.

The counselor in charge called the meeting to order: "Gentlemen, let's introduce ourselves. We have a new guest tonight."

That would be me.

Around the room they went with pained expressions, admitting "I'm _____ and I'm a turkey hunting addict. I'm here because I need help." Watching these grown men confess their addiction and subsequent need for professional help was slow and painful. The counselor beamed with each additional confession. I already didn't like him in a serious way. He was the only one not wearing camo. Everybody else had on hunting boots, but he wore penny loafers. I had this insane desire to jump across the room and jack slap that mule-eating-briars grin right off his face. Maybe I did need help.

My turn came. I swallowed hard, clinched my teeth, clasped

my hands together in a sweaty grip, and said in a barely audible whisper, "My name is Robert, and I'm a turkey hunting addict. I'm here because I need help."

I looked up and locked eyes with a 350-pound gorilla of a man with a giant beard down to his belly button. He slowly shook his head back and forth and mouthed, "No, no, no."

This was all the affirmation I needed. It was as if the Spirit of God sent an angel to visit me in the dungeon, so I kept talking. "Aw, shucks, who am I fooling? I don't need help. It's my wife who needs help. She is the one who made me come here — against my better judgment, I might add."

The guy on my right jumped up and shouted, "Me, too. My wife just doesn't understand me."

The guy on my left jumped up, slapped me on the back, and said, "My wife says dumb stuff such as 'You don't love me or the kids anymore. All you do is turkey hunt.' That's crazy talk. I can only turkey hunt for four to five weeks a year. The rest of the year, I stalk her around the house, and she doesn't even appreciate that."

Everybody laughed at that. The entire room was up now, talking and slapping each other on the back like long lost friends. Mr. Penny Loafer was standing on a chair trying to regain control, but without any success. The big man with the long beard looked at me and smiled as he slipped out the side door. Maybe he was an angel in disguise.

DEDICATION

This book is dedicated to all my turkey hunting friends, with whom I have shared many delightful hours of fellowship in the turkey woods. Some of you have taught me scouting/tracking and turkey/deer habits. Some of you have laughed with me and cried tears of frustration with me at our failures. Some have been jubilant at our shared successes. All of you have become my good friends. Collectively, our shared experiences are the stories I love to tell over and over. Thank you all for making mine a life full of a love for the great outdoors, a respect for the wild turkey, and a deep appreciation for lifelong friends.

Acknowledgements

This book would not have materialized without the kind assistance of my lovely bride, Mrs. Carlotta, who corrected my grammar and punctuation and provided many helpful insights. More than this, she is a fountain of biblical knowledge herself.

I am once again grateful for not only my friendship with Dr. Michael Cloer, pastor of Englewood Baptist Church in Rocky Mount, North Carolina, but also for his reading of this book at least twice in its roughest form to insure theological integrity.

I am indebted to Rob Keck, past CEO of National Wild Turkey Federation for twenty-seven years, for his technical advice regarding that most noble bird, the wild turkey. I do not have many people in my life who will provide brutally honest, constructive criticism about my writing. Rob Keck is one of those guys, and I value his input greatly.

Kudos to my daughter, Hannah Miller, for the front and back cover of this book. Once again, she hit a home run with eye-catching and nostalgic pictures with her photography skills.

I am also appreciative of the encouragement and patience of the staff at Baptist Courier Publishing, without whom this project would not have succeeded. Thank you, Rudy, Butch, and Denise! God bless you all!

FOREWORD

The return of the wild turkey across North America is one of the most remarkable conservation achievements ever known. With the restoration of this truly native all-American wildlife species has come the almost cult-like following of those who pursue this largest of game birds in both fall and spring of the year. The passion of these turkey hunters is only surpassed by their reverence for the bird, the sport, and their commitment of putting more back than they ever take away.

Turkey hunting is not only a national heritage in this country, it is a gift from God through creation; God is the designer of it all. When settlers first arrived on this continent, they found wildlife in great abundance, and that wildlife in turn fed a growing nation. People lived off the land and depended upon that wildlife for life itself. Unfortunately for most, they thought there was an endless supply, and by 1870 the wild turkey was gone from New England and most of the upper Midwest. By early in the twentieth century, those numbers were reduced to approximately 30,000 birds, with only scattered remnant flocks remaining.

Thanks to the foresight of Theodore Roosevelt, Gifford Pinchot, John Muir and others, the conservation movement was spawned, and the damage to our precious wildlife resources was reversed. Today we live in the Golden Years of the wild turkey and many other wildlife species, especially those that are hunted. Truly, the immense financial and in-kind contributions from hunters make them the unsung heroes of conservation.

This book, written by Dr. Robert Jackson, puts in perspective his more than three decades of personal turkey hunting experiences and illustrates them in relationship to the biblical records provided to all of God's people. Dr. Jackson's anecdotes share real life experiences from the field that uniquely illustrate how God expects us to live.

God reveals Himself through a variety of ways, but probably none better than through the splendor of the great outdoors. The spiritual nature of turkey hunters provides a closeness to our Creator and Savior maybe more than any other type of hunting pursuit. Dr. Jackson's abundant use of Scripture and tying it to his personal turkey hunting experiences gives us a strong foundation to understanding life itself. It would be an understatement to think that Christians enjoy the outdoors best because they first know our Creator. Turkey and non-turkey hunters alike will find refreshing answers to some of life's questions within the pages of this book.

— *Rob Keck*

The past Chief Executive Officer of the National Wild Turkey Federation for twenty-seven years and named one of "Hunting's 25 Most Influential Personalities of the 20ᵗʰ Century," Mr. Keck is currently the Director of Conservation for Bass Pro Shops, and he serves as Chairman of the Board of the Museum District of the Wonders of Wildlife National Museum and Aquarium. He has been the driving force in conservation on the national level for more than four decades, and during this time he built one of the most successful conservation organizations in the nation. He is currently serving as a deacon of Edgefield First Baptist Church in Edgefield, South Carolina.

The Family Doctor Speaks:

Turkey Tales
&
Bible Truths

1

A Twilight Encounter

The ranger at the Webb Center dropped me and my two friends, Harold and Jerry, off on a sandy road at the back of the state-controlled hunting preserve. The ranger was cordial. He had met us the evening before with a hot meal and plenty of hunting stories. Now it was barely daylight, and we tried to restrain our excitement at having drawn three Webb Center turkey hunts at the same time.

Harold was dropped off first. Before we had driven a quarter of a mile farther, his shotgun boomed. Jerry and I looked at each other with broad grins. These woods were full of gobblers. We discovered later that Harold had walked thirty yards into the woods, leaned against a tree, and yelped quietly. When he yelped, a gobbler flew down in front of him. He bagged his bird within ten minutes of walking into the woods. We were convinced we would all limit out by the end of the day.

Within an hour, it started drizzling rain. Within two hours, it was pouring. The rain didn't stop for two days. We saw neither hide nor hair — or should I say feather — of any turkey for two days. But we hunted hard despite the rain. After all, how often does a fella get drawn to hunt the Webb Center, famous for its turkey hunting. The ranger was apologetic, but he could not control the weather.

We were soaked through and through, cold and shivering, and disappointed. The second day, I jumped a swollen creek and fell backwards into the water — further soaking my already wet self and breaking the forearm on my shotgun in the process. I didn't know whether to cry, cuss, or laugh at my silly drenched self.

Two hours before time to leave on the last day, the rain stopped and the sun came out. I sat by a river bottom next to a large oak tree and nestled in some vines to hide myself, thinking this would be a good place for a turkey to roost — if they had ever gotten off the roost. A serpentine deer path, decorated with low-lying ferns on each side, meandered in front of me, snaking its way across the wooded river bottom.

I called softly a time or two, then settled back to wait and listen. I heard raindrops falling from the trees. A mist, rising from the river, glided silently beside me. The last rays of the sun pierced shafts of light through the semi-darkness of the evening shadows. Other than the occasional water drops, I heard no sound at all — not even a whisper of wind.

About 100 yards of dark green river bottom away, a sixty-pound doe timidly emerged from the shadows. She moved along the trail with her head down, stopping frequently to test the air and look to the right and to the left. She stopped with front and rear legs raised — frozen in position for long pauses

— and then resumed her slow progress, hiding occasionally behind the ferns. After walking through a shaft of sunlight, she disappeared into the shadow as if by magic, only to reappear a moment later.

I watched with keen interest as I realized her path ran beside my position. After thirty minutes, this pretty doe arrived at my outstretched boots, walked up to my knees, and stopped to stare at my camouflaged face.

My heart pounded in my chest and ears. I was twelve inches away from a wild deer and locked in a staring contest. I could smell her musty odor in the rain-washed atmosphere. The constriction and dilation of her dark pupils as she tried to make out my green net-covered features fascinated me. Her nostrils flared, absorbing the fragrance of man, which she must not have yet associated with danger. For the life of me, I don't know why my blinking eyes did not frighten her away. (Later, I remembered I had on tinted lens, which probably obscured my eyes.)

Knowing my shotgun lay across my lap, my bloodlust encouraged me to strike the side of her head swiftly, rendering her unconscious. After all, I am a deer hunter also. The moment was so surreal, so peaceful, and so friendly that I banished the thought. Then I had the crazy idea that I should just say, "Hey, my name is Robert. Do you come here often?" But I couldn't bring myself to spoil the magical moment. How many deer or turkey hunters do you know who have been close enough to a wild doe to smell her breath or kiss her lips?

After five minutes of staring at me like a coon in a tree,

she backed away without taking her eyes off me. Walking backwards, with her head down for the first thirty yards, she retraced her steps. Stopping to look over her shoulder to the right and to the left, she turned and walked away as slowly as she had come until she melted into the darkness on the far side of the river bottom. I realized my heart no longer pounded, but a cold sweat covered me, and I shivered in the evening chill.

Turkey hunting isn't just about bagging a big tom. It's about fellowship with good friends such as Harold and Jerry and about sharing stories like this one. It's about experiencing God's amazing creation, which He brought into existence by speaking a word, and about seeing the dogwood bloom deep in the turkey woods — knowing you and God are probably the only ones who enjoy its beauty. Turkey hunting is about pondering how "the heavens declare the glory of God" and how "the skies proclaim the work of His hands" (Psalm 19:1). It's about understanding that outdoorsmen know the truthfulness of that Scripture better than anyone else.

Turkey hunting helps us enjoy the wildlife God has put here for our pleasure. Perhaps one day, you, too, can stare deep into the eyes of a dark-eyed doe.

◆　◆　◆　◆　◆

Moses had a twilight encounter with God that lasted for forty days. God called him to the top of Mount Sinai, a mountain burning with fire and consumed with dark clouds, thunder, and lightning. The sight terrified the Israelites, and they wouldn't approach the mountain. Yet, God called Moses into the dark cloud to meet Him face-to-face. When Moses came down, his face radiated from beholding God's glory. The people were so frightened that they asked Moses to put a veil over his face. That encounter with God transformed Moses' entire life.

Moses wasn't always like that. He was raised in Pharaoh's house and was a prince in Egypt. One day, he came upon an Egyptian soldier beating a fellow Hebrew worker. Incensed, Moses struck and killed the Egyptian soldier. He then hid his body in the sand. When Moses' crime became public knowledge, he fled from Pharaoh's justice and wrath.

At that point, Moses was pridefully and heroically ready to help God's people, but God wasn't ready to use him. Moses had to spend the next forty years in the back desert of Midian, squeezing sand between his toes and listening to sheep bleat *baa! baa!* I'll bet that was good for his humility quotient.

Eventually, Moses had a surprise encounter with God at a burning bush. This event helped him get his head on straight. Between that encounter and spending forty days on Mount Sinai, Moses became known as the humblest man who ever lived: "Now Moses was a very humble man, more humble than anyone else on the face of the earth" (Numbers 12:3).

When we see God face-to-face, something happens that purges us of vain imaginations. True humility grows out of seeing ourselves as we really are, compared to a holy God as He is revealed in His perfect Word. If we spend enough time in God's Word seeking His face, God will cleanse us of pride and produce in us genuine humility.

Those encounters completely and forever changed Moses and the trajectory of his life. God could then use him to confront Pharaoh with a message that said, "Let my people go!" God also used Moses to perform great miracles in Egypt, calling forth ten plagues that ruined Egypt and led the Egyptians to drive the Hebrews out. After the deliverance, God used Moses to lead the stubborn and rebellious Israelites through forty years of wilderness wandering and finally to the entrance of the Promised Land. God also gave Moses the system of law and sacrifices that Israel followed for generations. Moses became known as the lawgiver. Statues and portraits of Moses holding the Ten Commandments adorn courtrooms all over the western world.

Where did this privileged position and notoriety come from? It came from a twilight encounter on a darkened mountain where Moses met with God, not as other men meet with God, as described in Numbers 12:8: "With him I speak face to face, clearly and not in riddles; he sees the form of the Lord."

You and I have twilight encounters with wildlife all the time, as I did with that little doe. Sometimes, it can be so stimulating that we talk about it for years. But have you ever had an encounter with the true and living God that radically changed your life? So much so that you can't stop talking about what Jesus did for you in that soul-cleansing, life-changing experience?

If so, "let the redeemed of the Lord say so" (Psalm 107:2 KJV). We don't need to have a shining face or two tablets of stone to set us apart from the crowd. All we need is a genuine account of once being dead in sin but now being made alive by the grace of God.

Put your humble shirt on, and let folks know you have had an encounter with the living God. Tell them the truth: "Once I was dead, but now I am alive. Once I was blind, but now I can see. Let me tell you how it all started. You see, I had this encounter with God …"

2

A Little Sand

We left the Webb Center — wet, cold, and disgusted. I threw my wet and sandy gear into my two-door, 1980s-model Chevy Blazer and headed home. My encounter with the little, dark-eyed doe was indelibly imprinted on my mind.

One week later, I was in Pacolet, South Carolina, hunting on the farm of my friend, Frank Mabry. The property belonged to his aunt and contained two ponds, large pastures, and deep hardwoods full of turkeys. The land was a turkey-hunting paradise for two amateur hunters, trying to learn the trade.

Before the season had begun, we roosted several toms and knew their whereabouts. We were pretty sure of the path they traveled to make their way into the pasture. A forty-yard-wide swath of hardwoods projected into the largest pasture, which was littered with droppings and scratchings at the base of the oak trees where they roosted. We planned to put a decoy in the pasture behind us, sit in the hardwoods that stuck out into the pasture, and intercept old tom after he flew down.

Saturday morning arrived, cold and wet after an overnight

rain. We drove in dense fog to the property. We set up in the fog, placing our hen decoy thirty yards out into the pasture. We sat against the large oak trees, thirty yards farther into the hardwoods facing the roosting trees. An eighteen-inch ground cover of heather with purple flowers soaked from the overnight rain surrounded us.

As soon as the sun pierced the dense fog, our gobbler sounded off multiple times in response to a soft tree call from my three-year-old box call. (At this point in my turkey hunting career, I could not reliably use a diaphragm mouth call without making horrible squeaking sounds that frightened both me and the turkey, so I stuck with my Quaker Boy box call.) I smiled all over. I loved it when a plan came together. Frank was behind me, facing the decoy and sitting under some low-lying cedar limbs on the edge of the pasture.

Turkeys have excellent vision, but I couldn't see thirty yards in front of me because of the dense fog and early morning twilight. Somehow, through the fog and the darkness, that old tom saw the decoy from 150 to 200 yards away. The next thing I knew, he flew over me, landed in the pasture behind me beside the decoy, gobbled twice, and commenced to parading in a full strut beside that hen decoy.

I looked over my shoulder and saw Frank mesmerized by the entire spectacle. I couldn't tell if he was asleep or frozen like Hercules after beholding Medusa. I couldn't stand it. I rolled onto my belly and army-crawled thirty yards to the edge of the woods, getting completely soaked by the wet heather. But I didn't care about getting wet. A gobbler in full strut begged to be bagged, and my partner was under the spell of a sorceress. (Please don't follow my example. Army crawling through the woods during turkey season with a firearm is a good way to get shot or to shoot yourself.)

I put the bead of my 12-gauge Remington 1100 with the broken forearm on the glowing white head of Mr. Tom, which was luminescent against the backdrop of the dense gray fog. But I — couldn't — push — the — safety — off!! I panicked. This turkey had strutted and gobbled for ten to fifteen minutes by now. Out of the corner of my eye, I saw Frank — still paralyzed. In my mind, I screamed, *Frank, shoot, shoot!*

I laid the gun down and crawled backwards to my initial position by the big oak tree, further drenching my already-soaked hunting clothes. I took out a shotgun shell and surreptitiously beat on the safety. It wouldn't budge. I spit on it several times. I tried to pry it with my hunting knife. No success. On the verge of tears, I looked over my shoulder. My gobbler was walking off in full strut across that large pasture, leaving my hen forlorn and Frank under the cedar tree frozen in place. He gobbled one last time just to spite me before disappearing over the horizon.

I slumped against the oak tree — cold, wet, lonesome, and frustrated. I wondered why I loved turkey hunting so much. I could have been home by my lovely bride — warm in bed, comfortable, and happy. Why do I do this to myself?

As I sat beside that big oak tree, I recalled how I had fallen backwards into the creek at the Webb Center and how I had thrown my wet and sandy gear into the back of my truck. I had broken a fundamental rule of hunting: Always clean your firearm. Webb Center sand — like a bad souvenir — lodged in my safety. My carelessness had foiled my careful plans and cost me a big tom turkey.

Every military man has had a drill instructor who screamed at him, "Clean your weapon. Keep your weapon clean. Your life depends on it." And the DI was right. In the heat and grime of battle, a clean, well-oiled firearm may mean the difference between life and death. A little grit can keep a firearm from functioning properly, as I learned to my regret and Tom's delight that cold and wet April morning.

◆　◆　◆　◆　◆

Christians are instruments in the Lord's hands, implements of righteousness (Romans 6:13). A surgeon does not operate with non-sterile instruments, a cook does not cook with unsanitary cookware, and men do not want tools without fine edges in their shops. Holy Spirit cannot effectively use a dirty vessel that contains the sand of sin where the oil of Holy Spirit should be lubricating our lives and making us function powerfully and effectively in the kingdom of God.

When I was a child, I had a toy railroad — the old kind with metal tracks and heavy metal engines and cars, with none of the plastic and rubber parts used nowadays. I loved to set it up in my mother's living room and surround it with my army soldiers, tanks, and forts.

One day, I couldn't get my train to operate. I examined the

track. Everything was connected. With the transformer also connected properly and the wall plug in place, I was mystified. Then, I discovered a metal railroad-crossing sign had fallen across the track, short-circuiting the entire system. All the electrical power of South Carolina Electric and Gas could not operate that little train system because of one little railroad crossing sign.

Unconfessed sin is like that metal railroad-crossing sign. It short-circuits the power of Almighty God in our lives. He will not effectively use us as unsanitary, non-sterile, and unclean instruments. Notice, I said "unconfessed sin."

We all have sin in our lives. The question is what we do with it. We can ignore the conviction of Holy Spirit regarding our sin, or we can immediately confess and repent. We can coddle sin in our heart, or we can turn our back on it in genuine repentance. Isaiah the prophet said, "But your iniquities have separated you from your God; your sins have hidden his face from you, so that he will not hear" (Isaiah 59:2).

Sin always separates us from God, our family, and our friends. We should deal with it as severely as a surgeon deals with cancer. Cut it out of our lives. When doctors give cancer patients the option of curative surgery or other less-effective treatments, they almost always say, "Doctor, take it out. I want surgery."

We can turn to Holy Spirit and say, "Take it away. I repent. I'm never going back." God honors repentant attitudes and gives grace and spiritual strength to live a holy and pure life. "For God did not call us to be impure but to live a holy life"

(1 Thessalonians 4:7). God never calls us to do something He doesn't give us power to do. The grace of God and the power of Holy Spirit enables us to live a pure and holy life.

Is there any sand of sin in your life? Any grit you need to confess and repent of before you can be a clean vessel in the hands of the Lord. "Repent, then, and turn to God, so that your sins may be wiped out, that times of refreshing may come from the Lord" (Acts 3:19).

◆　◆　◆　◆　◆

I know you are wondering what happened to Frank. I sprinkled him with monkey dust and rescued him from the sorceress's spell. "Frank, why didn't you shoot?" I asked in exasperation. "That turkey strutted thirty yards in front of you."

He looked at me and smiled, "This was your hunt and your gobbler. You planned the entire hunt. I wanted you to shoot that bird."

I stared at him in disbelief. I knew I didn't have that kind of unselfishness in me. I didn't care whose hunt it was. I would have blasted that bird to turkey heaven. But that was Frank. He was everybody's friend. He would stand in the rain and hold a bucket for you if you asked him. He would give you the shirt off his back. He was always buying me turkey calls and turkey gear just because I was his friend. I backed over a cheap box call with my truck one Saturday morning, and the next week Frank brought me a new one. That was Frank.

Frank went to be with Jesus a few years ago — prematurely.

Everybody misses him because he was everybody's friend. I've never hunted that turkey paradise in Pacolet again. I could probably ask his kinfolk for permission, but it wouldn't be the same without my good turkey-hunting friend. Funny thing about turkey hunting — half the joy is sharing the experience with a good friend. But you already know that, don't you?

Harold's Deep-Fried Turkey Breast

Remove both breasts from a recently harvested wild turkey.

Inject both breasts with Tony Chachere's Creole Butter Injectable Marinade.

Let sit for twenty to thirty minutes.

Heat oil to 300 degrees.

Deep fry until golden brown, usually fifteen minutes per breast.

Usually sliced and served with an electric knife in ¼-inch slices as an appetizer, since it doesn't last long enough for a meal.

(Photo by Randy Fath, Unsplash.com)

3

My First Hunt

"Most places we know have a whole generation of hunters that have never fall turkey hunted and know little about it … The point I would make with all this is undoubtedly the greatest challenge in turkey hunting is pursuing wise old gobblers in the fall."

— Legends of the Fall *by Larry Case*

The phone rang at 3:00 a.m. A friend on the other end said, "Let's go turkey hunting."

"There are no turkeys around here. Are you crazy?"

"Sure, there are. The woods are full of them," he said confidently.

I raised up and looked out the darkened window and saw pouring rain. Automatically, I responded, "It's raining."

"Best time to hunt. Let's go."

I don't know what possessed me, but I got out of bed at 3:00 a.m. and dressed. My wife mumbled, "What are you doing?"

"I'm going turkey hunting."

"Oh, ok," she said and rolled over like this was normal behavior for me.

I'd never hunted anything but quail and dove in high school. I was as blind as a bat back then and didn't know it until I applied for my driver's license at age seventeen. By then, I was sick of hunting with my dad, who would get his limit every time. I would do well to get two birds with two boxes of shells. It was humiliating, so I stuck with basketball.

I rummaged in the closet for my hunting gear: my high school letter jacket, tennis shoes, and my dad's dark green Vietnam-era plastic raincoat which hung to my ankles. I had saved his air commando hat, which was a size too small and sat on my head like a beanie. But it was camouflaged and was all I had that resembled hunting gear. I had my dad's Remington 1100 12- gauge, and my friend gave me some turkey shells. We loaded up in my turkey hunting vehicle — a 1977 burgundy Monte Carlo with shiny spoked rims, a sweet ride.

We arrived on the edge of public hunting land at Cross Anchor, South Carolina, and waited for daylight. The car windows fogged as we watched and waited. While we sat waiting, I asked my friend, "How much do you really know about turkey hunting?"

He responded confidently, "Plenty."

I asked, "How many times have you been turkey hunting?"

Looking out the side window, he answered, "A couple."

That gave me a great deal of reassurance.

Finally, my friend said, "The rain has slacked up. Let's go."

He jumped out of the car, and I watched through the passenger window as he disappeared into the darkness. Sadly, my friend was mistaken. The rain still poured like Noah's flood from the floodgates of heaven.

I grabbed my turkey gun from the back seat, opened the door, and stepped into two feet of cold water, flooding my tennis shoes in the process. My first turkey hunt was not going well. I took off, sloshing through the darkness after my disappearing friend. I caught up to him, and we stood under a pine tree until we saw daylight. We then tiptoed through the tulips … no, pine trees … over a dense mat of wet pine needles.

Suddenly, my friend grabbed my arm, pointed near a tree, and whispered, "Turkey. Shoot."

I looked and, through the rainwater on my glasses, saw an ill-defined dark object standing next to some tree limbs about twenty yards away. It didn't look like a turkey. It really didn't look like anything.

Again, my friend said, "Shoot."

Hesitating a few seconds, I dutifully raised my shotgun and pointed at the object. (Looking back on this, I have realized how unsafe it was for me to point my firearm at a poorly identified object.) At the same time, a long-feathered neck unraveled from under a wing and looked around with black, penetrating eyes, finally landing on me. The feathers on his neck were soaking wet. I realized then this really was a turkey, and he looked more miserable than I was.

"Shoot!"

I shot and put him out of his misery. The turkey fell over,

and I had my first jake. Boy, was I thrilled! We thought it was a hen until some more experienced hunters told us how to tell them apart by pulling back the feathers on the jake's chest, which revealed a short, little beard. (This occurred in the early 1980s when South Carolina had a fall season when one could shoot either a hen or a gobbler.) I was puffed up and proud. I fell in love with turkey hunting that day, even though I never heard a gobbler or saw a gobbler strut. I thought, This turkey hunting is great fun and easy.

I knew nothing about calling turkeys and owned no turkey calls, so I quickly bought real hunting gear, including turkey calls. I listened to audio tapes and went to seminars on turkey hunting and calling. I read every magazine and book available. I hunted hard for three years, calling up lots of birds, but never bagging a one. So much for this being easy. Three long years passed before I bagged a long beard. As they say, pride goes before a dry spell.

♦　♦　♦　♦　♦

I suppose you know where this is heading. Just as I was foolish enough to think turkey hunting was easy, so we Christians are often foolish enough to think the Christian life is easy, too. But why should we when we know we face such serious enemies as the world, the flesh, and Satan? Let's look at these individually.

The world — A world system out there thinks differently than we do. They ask, "How could you shoot something that beautiful? That's cruel." Yet, at the same time, they would advocate for the aborting of unborn babies. Go figure. If the world had its way, hunting turkey and deer would be illegal.

The world is that ordered system headed by Satan who intentionally opposes God and His kingdom. Satan is referred to as the "god of this world" (2 Corinthians 4:4 NASB). Adam and Eve originally held the title deed to this world, but because of their sin they forfeited ownership over to Satan, who became the new owner. Because of sin and its abusive new owner, the world groans until the day of its redemption (Romans 8:22). That's why we experience sickness, disease, death, and natural disasters.

My patients often ask me why they have inexplicable diseases. I tell them because we are all sinners. Sometimes, they get it; sometimes, they don't. The original owners were slack and let the world slip into the hands of a new landowner. That is why it was no empty promise when Satan tempted Jesus in the wilderness by showing Him all the kingdoms of the world in an instant and then said, "I will give you all their authority and splendor, for it has been given to me, and I can give it to anyone I want to. So, if you worship me, it will all be yours" (Luke 4:5-7).

Whether we admit it or not, Satan rules over all the institutions of man (1 John 5:19b). They are all secular and opposed to God and His kingdom: governments, the United Nations, the military, the educational system, and the media. All are institutions that in some way oppose the kingdom of God as represented by His church. Tension will always exist between the agencies of the state and the church, which represents God and morality.

In John 17, Jesus prayed, "I pray for them. I'm not praying for the world but for those you have given me." Jesus distinguishes His disciples from the rest of the world's population. He continues, "I have given them your word and the world has hated them, for they are not of the world any more than I am of the world. My prayer is not that You take them out of the world but that You protect them from the evil one. They are not of the world, even as I am not of it."

Jesus talks about another system. He declares that He is not of this world system and neither are His disciples. They belong to God's invisible kingdom. He later told Pilate, "My kingdom is not of this world."

Believers walk in this world, live in this world, and work in this world, but we are not of this world's system. "Our citizenship is in heaven" (Philippians 3:20). We are passing through as pilgrims and sojourners. The world hated Jesus, and He warned us it would hate us, too. Where do we get off thinking that life would be easy as a Christian?

The flesh — When I hunt, I sometimes get tired and a little sleepy. I want to lay my head against a tree, close my eyes, and sleep a little — rather than stay alert as I should. A friend of mine fell asleep while turkey hunting, and a raccoon walked up and punched him in the chest, leaving a perfect red clay paw print on his chest. He opened his eyes, freaking out the raccoon who immediately fled. The raccoon unnerved my friend, and his friends never tired of laughing at him.

The spirit is willing, but the flesh is weak and is not our friend. Paul writes, "For when we were controlled by the sinful nature, the sinful passions aroused by the law were at work in our bodies, so that we bore fruit for death. But now, by dying to what once bound us, we have been released from the law so that we serve in the new way of the Spirit, and not in the old way of the written code" (Romans 7:5-6).

The flesh, often called the lower nature, loves to sin and rebel against God and His law. If we give in to the flesh, we head towards death. Sin in us activates and energizes our flesh. Becoming a believer does not eradicate the evil desires of the flesh. We all recognize that. Paul wrote in Galatians 5:16-21:

> *So I say, live by the Spirit, and you will not gratify the desires of the sinful nature. For the sinful nature desires what is contrary to the Spirit, and the Spirit what is contrary to the sinful nature. They are in conflict with each other, so that you do not do what you want. But if you are led by the Spirit, you are not under law. The acts of the sinful nature are obvious: sexual immorality, impurity and debauchery; idolatry and witchcraft, hatred, discord, jealousy, fits of rage, selfish ambition, dissensions, factions and envy; drunkenness, orgies, and the like. I warn you, as I did before, that those who live like this will not inherit the kingdom of God.*

Because Holy Spirit lives in us, we can walk in the Spirit and not fulfill the desires of our lower nature. The Spirit and the flesh do constant battle, keeping us from consistently choosing good and right things. Then Paul lists the works of the flesh, which is a disheartening description of corrupt deeds men do when guided by their lower nature. Christian people can participate in these awful, sinful deeds even though indwelt by Holy Spirit. The influence of the flesh is powerful. If we don't put to death the desires of the flesh daily, then we end up in that list.

When my children were small, my wife and I taught them the concept of the spirit-controlled life versus the flesh-controlled life. At times, I saw them struggle to obey us. I would catch their attention, take a symbolic knife in my right hand, stab myself in the heart, and grimace painfully, indicating death to self. They would smile as they grasped the concept, sometimes imitating the maneuver and swiftly obeying. They understood the death to self we as adults struggle so hard to practice.

Jesus said, "If anyone would come after me, he must deny himself and take up his cross daily and follow me" (Luke 9:23). We may have to stick that spiritual dagger in our heart dozens of times each day to fully crucify the flesh.

But the beauty of the crucified life is that we look less like ourselves and more like Jesus every day. The flesh dissipates and Jesus shines through brighter and brighter. We produce the fruit of the Spirit. "But the fruit of the Spirit is love, joy, peace, patience, kindness, goodness, faithfulness, gentleness, and self-control. Against such things there is no law. Those who belong to Christ Jesus have crucified the sinful nature with its passions and desires. Since we live by the Spirit, let us keep in step with the Spirit" (Galatians 5:22-25).

As we daily crucify the flesh with its passions and desires, Holy Spirit produces sweet and precious fruit in our lives that makes us look, talk, and walk like Jesus. Paul says, "For if you live according to the sinful nature, you will die; but if by the Spirit you put to death the misdeeds of the body, you will live" (Romans 8:13).

Satan — Have you ever scouted before turkey season opens and found a gobbler in full strut? Your mind screams, "Shoot him. Clean him. Nobody will know." Where does that come from? The father of lies. The devil himself. Scripture teaches us that Satan belonged to the order of angels called cherubim (Ezekiel 28:14). He is described as "the model of perfection, full of wisdom and perfect in beauty" (Ezekiel 28:12). Verse 15 says of him, "You were blameless in your ways from the day you were created 'til wickedness was found in you."

Unlike God, who is the creator and is eternal, Satan is a created being with limitations. God created him blameless, perfect, and beautiful, but he became the wicked, lying, murderous creature he is now. But how?

One day in heaven, despite Satan's privileged position and perfect environment, pride entered his heart. He lusted after God's place of authority, saying in his heart, "I will make myself like the Most High" (Isaiah 14:14). Knowing immediately what His highest-ranking official was thinking in his heart — and His eyes being "too pure to look on evil" (Habakkuk 1:13)

— God immediately cast Satan, and one third of the angels who followed him in his rebellion, out of heaven and down to earth. Like a lightning bolt, God excommunicated Satan. "God opposes the proud but gives grace to the humble" (James 4:6).

Like turkey hunting, the Christian life is difficult. Satan doesn't make it easy, as Charles Ryrie states:

- He tempts us to lie like Ananias and Sapphira (Acts 5:3).
- He accuses and slanders you and me (Revelation 12:10).
- He hinders our work for God as he did Paul in his ministry (1 Thessalonians 2:18).
- He employs his underlings to defeat us (Ephesians 6:11-12).
- He tempts us to immorality (1 Corinthians 7:5).
- He sows tares among believers to deceive and confuse (Matthew 13:38-39).
- He even incites persecution against believers (Revelation 2:10).
- More than that, he is always trying to get us to follow a counterfeit plan of doing good rather than doing the best. (Summarized from *A Survey of Bible Doctrine* by Charles C. Ryrie, Chicago: Moody Press, 1972, p. 95)

Anytime Satan can divert us from the main thing, which is sharing the gospel and making disciples, he wins and we lose. So, what's a Christian turkey hunter to do? Hey, Brother, you

don't go turkey hunting without your camouflage and turkey
vest, do you?

1. Don't leave your house any day without putting on the
    full armor of God, as outlined in Ephesians 6:11-18.
    Each piece of armor has its purpose and should be put
    on prayerfully.
2. "Resist the devil and he will flee from you" (James 4:7).
    We must take a decisive stand against Satan in our lives.
3. Keep a proper respect for our enemy. Even though
    God's power is on our side, victory is not guaranteed.
    Our flesh is weak, and our enemy is full of guile.
4. Be fully informed of Satan's tactics and always alert, for
    "your enemy the devil prowls around like a roaring lion
    looking for someone to devour" (1 Peter 5:8). (Points
    one through four summarized from *A Survey of Bible
    Doctrine* by Charles C. Ryrie, Chicago: Moody Press,
    1972, pp. 95-96)

Being a Christian is not a turkey shoot. We have too many
enemies: the world, the flesh, and Satan. Remember the "reason
the Son of God appeared was to destroy the devil's work" (1
John 3:8). More than that, He has overcome the world on our
behalf. By God's Spirit in us, we can put to death the desires of
the flesh.

At the conclusion of the last turkey hunting seminar I
attended, the event organizer challenged us to bag a big ole'
tom. At the conclusion of this lesson, let me challenge you to

walk in victory over the world, the flesh, and Satan. Doing so may not be easy, but God has made it possible "because greater is He who is in [us] than he who is in the world" (1 John 4:4 NASB).

4

Blind Spots

I prayed for my three-year drought to end. I had hunted hard during those years, but had not bagged a single tom. I had taken several shots and either clean missed or lost a wounded bird, which always made me heart sick. My friend and hunting buddy, Chip, determined to help me end this sorry chapter in my life.

Mid-morning, we sat with our backs against some mature pine trees when the first bird of the day gobbled — really close. I shivered with cold and excitement. Chip called quietly with his mouth call, and that bird double-gobbled so loud and so close that my heart leaped into my throat. I scanned the woods in front of me, looking for any sign of movement. Nothing moved. No sound. Twenty minutes moved by slowly when, *de novo,* out of nothing, a turkey in full strut emerged from behind a large pine tree not fifty yards away. With mincing steps, he slowly pranced to within forty yards, perfect range for my 12-gauge pump shotgun.

My heart pounded and my breathing quickened. I told

myself, "Put the stock firmly against your shoulder and cheek. Line up front and rear sights. Don't jerk the trigger." Unfortunately, that morning I had put on a new woolen camo head covering to keep my head and neck warm. At that moment, it slipped over my mouth, and my heavy breathing fogged up both lenses of my glasses. I entered panic mode, but I couldn't move a muscle lest I frighten my gobbler. He strutted forty yards away and danced himself closer to a mid-morning breakfast of hot lead, but I was blinded. I tried tipping my head down and looking over my glasses, but I'm near-sighted. All I could see was brown and green blurs in the distance — nothing I could distinguish as a tom turkey.

I heard Chip whisper from twenty yards away, "Shoot. Shoot."

Paralyzed, I turned my head slowly from side to side. I discovered a thin sliver of clear glass in the upper middle on both sides against my nose. Holding my breath to prevent further fogging, I tilted my head down until I could see through that little sliver. I found the turkey, which was now thirty yards away, and sent him to turkey heaven as I heard Chip almost shout, "Shoot!"

My three-year drought ended. Chip and I were elated. We whooped and hollered for ten minutes. My gobbler had a 9½-inch beard and weighed eighteen pounds. I was excited. I had to call all my friends on my bag phone. (Before cell phones existed, I had a bag phone in my truck as big as Strong's Exhaustive Concordance and just about as heavy.)

Chip scolded me, "Why didn't you shoot? I thought you

were going to let that bird walk up your gun barrel."

"Brother, I was blinded. My glasses fogged up completely, and I couldn't see a thing. He almost got away because I was blinded."

◆　◆　◆　◆　◆

Blind spots can prove fatal, especially when driving a vehicle. Blind spots in our lives can be harmful to relationships. Here's the hard part: We all have them. Things about ourselves we cannot perceive. Things about our character our wives and friends see clearly, but we don't see at all.

I had several issues in my personal life (none of your business) my wife kept pointing out to me over the years of our marriage. I disagreed with her that these things were problematic. At times, we debated these things heatedly. At other times, we discussed them in congenial adult fashion. Sometimes, we fought like barnyard dogs fighting over table scraps. In the end, I didn't see it the way she did, and we were at an impasse. She was often quite perturbed. I was unperturbed because I was blind to the seriousness of my character flaws and how they affected my wife — and just as importantly, my testimony.

Over time, she stopped discussing these things with me anymore, nor did she get emotionally upset anymore. She merely resorted to saying things such as, "You'll never change. I don't know why I even try anymore." I suppose I should have been happy when she said that because it meant she was going to leave me alone. But for some reason, her statement flew all over me and made me mad. Our relationship deteriorated.

I knew I was the spiritual leader and needed to do something. For two years, I prayed God would take us to the next level in our marriage and in our spiritual relationship. Then God took the blinders off my eyes. He showed me nobody loved me as much as my wife, and nobody would risk telling me the truth about myself as much or as often as she would. Next, He showed me that much of the time she had been right, and I had been wrong about the issues in my life. What were they? Like I said, none of your business, but probably pretty much the same as yours.

Honestly, I was ashamed. For a while, I was mad at God, but I got over it. I was too proud and embarrassed to admit to my wife that she had been right all along. Eventually, I took my precious, long-suffering wife on a weekend retreat, got on my knees, and confessed fifteen years of wrong-doing and spiritual blindness. I admitted she was right over multiple specific issues, and I promised to do better. Her response? Skepticism. But she withheld judgment, even though I didn't have a good track record.

For the next three months, things were touch and go as I shifted to a new lifestyle — the new me. I messed up a few times and had to apologize. For example, I had a bad habit of spending money without asking my wife — not large amounts, but just on dumb stuff. One day, I came home with $300 worth of baby bream and catfish to put in our pond in the horse pasture. Although not a huge sum of money, I had agreed not to spend even that much money without consulting my wife. I was excited about plans to stock the horse pasture pond until I saw my baby's face. Then I remembered. What was I thinking? I wasn't thinking. I was being my old self. I had broken my promise. I was embarrassed once again and had to beg forgiveness and start all over. What a dummy. Blind spots die hard.

After three months of struggling, she said, "You were serious, weren't you?"

"About what?" I asked.

"About changing your life and getting rid of the blind spots."

"Yes, ma'am, I was, and I am serious."

"Well, you're doing a great job," she said.

Since then, a new day has dawned in our marriage. In our social life, we don't walk around on eggshells anymore. Nor are we overly careful about what we say. We can pray and minister together without underlying resentments or misunderstandings. A new day also dawned in other areas — if you know what I mean.

The Bible tells men we should "live with [our] wives in an understanding way" (1 Peter 3:7 NASB). That means we can't look at our guy friends any longer with exasperation and say, "Women, who can understand them?" and hear them give a sarcastic laugh.

Our wives think differently, and it should be our lifelong quest to comprehend their minds and emotions. More than that, it is our responsibility to treat them with respect and honor, even when they take it upon themselves to point out our blind spots. Nobody else loves us enough to tell us the truth about ourselves. Not the guys at work, our kids, or our mamas. Only our loving brides.

What's our response? We can bow up with anger in protest as I did for fifteen years, or we can put on our humble shirt and say, "Precious, I appreciate your input. I will pray about it. I don't quite see it that way, but I trust that God speaks to me through you, so I will give it some serious consideration."

We would probably rather a herd of wild buffalo run over us than to say those words to our wives, especially after they have been pointing out our character flaws, but "God opposes the proud but gives grace to the humble" (James 4:6). More than that, Peter says if we don't live with our wives in an understanding way our prayers may go unanswered (1 Peter 3:7).

Oh well, that explains a lot. No wonder God hasn't been answering our prayers. We have been bowing up and angry with Mama for years over our blind spots. Better be careful. Remember my turkey that almost got away because I was blinded? I know a man whose wife got away because he was blind, and after she was gone, all he could say was, "What was her issue?"

Don't be that guy. I'm thankful God opened my eyes and showed me my blind spots. I don't care if you must pray every day for two years for God to take your marriage to the next level. I don't care if you find out your blind spots are the problem in your marriage. Pray every day that God would reveal the blind spots in your life. Be grateful if He uses someone who loves you as much as your wife, rather than a marriage counselor or the judge in divorce court.

"You husbands likewise, live with your wives in an understanding way, as with a weaker vessel, since she is a woman; and grant her honor as a fellow heir of the grace of life, so that your prayers may not be hindered" (1 Peter 3:7 NASB).

(Photo by Suzy Brooks, Unsplash.com)

5

BE PREPARED

On a cold April morning, I set out for my friend Randy's farm. He was a pharmaceutical rep with a small farm on Highway 146 between Woodruff, South Carolina, and Cross Anchor. The land was uniquely situated against 500 acres of game management land that no one seemed to hunt except for me, and it was loaded with turkeys begging to go home in my game bag. I could gain access to this GMA through his little farm.

On this Saturday morning, Randy had gone to Atlanta, Georgia, on a business trip. I arrived before daylight and opened the door of my Chevy Blazer. Immediately, I heard two gobblers sound off across his horse pasture. My heart pounded, and I saw myself smiling in the rearview mirror. I quietly slipped to the back of my truck, lifted the gate, and put on my turkey vest. I removed my freshly cleaned and oiled shotgun and felt around in the darkness for my box of #5 turkey shells. I patted the carpet in the darkness, but couldn't find the box. Another turkey gobbled, and slow panic seeped into the edges of my consciousness.

I ran my hands all over the carpet in the back of my truck. Nothing. I quick walked to the cab and felt in the console and under the seat. Still, nothing. By now, I was sweating. Another turkey double gobbled. I looked down at the horse pasture while full-blown panic started to overwhelm me. I glanced at Randy's house, thinking, I know it's indecent to wake him at this early hour, but surely he will have some shells. Then I remembered he was in Atlanta.

I slumped against the side of my truck as two gobblers pirouetted in full strut in the middle of the horse pasture. The early morning sun lit up the iridescent colors of the turkeys' outstretched feathers.

Then, I awakened with a start, sat straight up in my bed with genuine sweat on my neck, and realized I had dreamed. A bad dream. Really, a nightmare. My heart was beating so fast and I was breathing so hard that my wife asked, "Baby, are you okay?"

I responded, "No, not really. I just messed up a really great turkey hunt."

Unprepared. We've all been that way at one time or another. We've all arrived in the woods only to realize we left our rifle cartridges on the bedroom dresser, our broadheads on the work bench, or our hunting license in our other coat.

One year, a friend and I were on our way to the Savannah River deer hunt, thirty miles from my home, driving in the dark, drinking coffee, talking, and looking forward to the hunt for which we had been drawn when my friend suddenly shouted, "My license! I left my hunting license!"

Our leisurely drive turned into a NASCAR event as we turned around, drove hard to Spartanburg, retrieved his license, made up time retracing our steps, explained to an understanding highway patrolman in some small town why we were burning up the road, and finally got through the gate three minutes late. Don't look so smug. I know you have been there and done that, too.

I left work one day to hunt on a piece of property near Woodruff, South Carolina, that one of my patients owned. I got out of my medical office clothes, put on my camo, and realized I had left my hunting boots at home. Chagrined, I put my nice, shiny loafers back on, hoisted my climbing stand onto my back, gathered my compound bow, and started walking.

All was well until I came to a large mud puddle in the middle of the mud road with a neat little grass strip down the middle, which I commenced to tightrope. Halfway through, I lost my balance. One of my shiny loafers sank into the red mud and disappeared. When I pulled my foot up, the loafer stayed down. I stood there with a climbing stand on my back, a bow in hand, my right leg curled under me like a stork and balanced precariously, wondering what to do. I squatted on one leg, keeping my socked foot curled up, reached into the mud until I found my loafer and pulled it out. I put the muddy shoe back on and said to myself, "What the heck." Then, I walked through the muddy water the rest of the way. It didn't really matter because it poured down rain about an hour later, and I missed a straight down shot at fifteen yards on a four-point buck — a miserable day all around. Unprepared. Ever been there?

One day at my office, a strange man walked through the parking lot, grabbed a female patient as she exited her vehicle, groped her, and ran off. Another male patient witnessed the event and chased the perpetrator. The only problem was that when he left home to drive his wife to the doctor's office he was wearing his pajamas and two-foot-long pink bunny slippers — and with really big ears.

The perpetrator had on tennis shoes and left the witness in the dust. I knew nothing about this until I went to the kitchen for a mid-morning break and found two police officers interviewing a patient in pajamas and two-foot-long pink bunny slippers with really big ears. The patient sat there with his legs crossed while those pink slippers dominated the kitchen. I thought he had done something wrong. I mean, the police were interrogating him, and he was dressed rather unusually. I thought he had to be the perpetrator, but he was the unprepared witness. Just like us when we go hunting without our shells, flashlight, or license. (Remember my patient the next time you drive your wife or kids somewhere with your pajamas and bunny slippers on ☺.)

◆　◆　◆　◆　◆

When my son Rob was in high school, he carried a backpack everywhere he went with an odd assortment of equipment in it. Everything from a Leatherman utility tool to a pocketknife, a lighter, Chapstick, Band-Aids, duct tape, flashlights, and small screwdrivers. On top of that, he was a handyman who could fix anything and delighted in doing it. If anyone needed a screw tightened or a child's abrasion bandaged, they cried, "Where's Rob?" Everyone knew he was prepared.

In 1 Peter 3:15 (NASB), the apostle Peter told his readers to "sanctify Christ as Lord in your hearts, always being ready to make a defense to everyone who asks you to give an account for the hope that is in you, yet with gentleness and reverence." In essence, he instructed them to prepare to defend their faith.

Have people ever asked you questions about the Christian life, ethics, or the Bible that left you stumped or confused? My patients ask me hard questions all the time. "Dr. Jackson, why did God take my child away with that dreaded leukemia?" "Why did God let my husband abandon me with these three children and no job?" "Why do I have to suffer this terrible pain every day of my life?" "Why am I so depressed all the time? My life is great. There's no reason for me to be depressed."

Our children and co-workers might ask us such questions. When we get these kinds of questions, we need to have the right size shells in our turkey vests. If we aren't prepared, our camo better be good so we can hide.

Turkey hunters prepare before turkey season by scouting out their favorite hunting spots, practicing with their turkey calls, patterning their shotgun and shells, and checking their camo, license, and tags. Only foolish hunters prepare the night before opening day.

How do we prepare ourselves to give an answer and a defense to those who ask about the hope we have within us?

Begin by studying the word. Paul said, "Study to show

thyself approved unto God, a workman that needeth not to be ashamed, rightly dividing the Word of truth" (2 Timothy 2:15 KJV). No substitute or shortcut exists for self-study of God's Word. People ask me where I went to Bible school. I laughingly tell them I went to KTBS: Kitchen Table Bible School. All my Bible training came from every day reading of the Word, studying the Bible, and memorizing Scripture at my kitchen table. I also try to listen to good Bible teaching on the radio and read good Christian books. I also determined in my heart a long time ago to be a good Bible teacher (Ezra 7:10).

Attend a Bible teaching church where you can be instructed in the Word and equipped for every good service. Be faithful in attending a Bible study class where you can ask hard questions and get good answers.

Commit to memorizing a verse of Scripture every week. Colossians 3:16 reads, "Let the word of Christ dwell in you richly as you teach and admonish one another with all wisdom." Answering hard questions comes easy when you have God's Word in your heart.

Read a book on apologetics, such as Alex McFarland's book, *The Ten Most Common Objections to Christianity*. I know most of you guys probably haven't read a complete book since you graduated from high school, so get your wife to read a chapter to you every day. For those of you who want more substantial and deeper apologetics, I recommend *Evidence That Demands a Verdict* by Josh McDowell, the Answers series edited by Ken Ham with *Answers in Genesis*, or Lee Strobel's books.

Stop listening to country music and talk radio and listen

to good Bible teaching on the radio or podcasts while driving or working if permissible. Some of the best Bible teachers in America are available on radio and podcasts if we just tune in. I de-double-dog dare you.

Learn a three-minute evangelistic testimony. Write out your testimony: your life before Christ, how you met Christ, and your life after coming to know Christ. Finish with one verse of Scripture, and then memorize it. You will be surprised at how God gives you opportunities to share that testimony once you are prepared.

Be familiar with a gospel presentation, whether it is a gospel tract or an electronic version such as the Three Circles: Life Conversation Guide application. Learning a gospel presentation by heart opens many opportunities to share the gospel. Preparation and opportunity often intersect.

Just as we cannot bag a big tom turkey if we are unprepared — or if we are sitting in our recliner, flipping through the hunting channels on our remote — neither can we be good at defending our faith if we are not prepared. I have friends who have all the latest turkey calls and the newest camo, but they never get into the woods to turkey hunt. I also have Christian friends who go to evangelism conferences and apologetics conferences and own all the latest evangelistic and apologetics books and CDs. However, they never attempt to share with anybody "a defense of the hope that is in them with gentleness and reverence."

Before I leave for the turkey woods, I run through a mental check list. Do I have my license? Do I have my shells, my camo, my calls? You probably do the same thing. In fact, you've probably had the same nightmare I had when I dreamed of leaving my shells behind. That's almost as bad as dreaming of showing up at church in just your underwear. Don't tell me you've never had that nightmare.

Any kind of hunting takes a lot of preparation — all for a turkey or a deer that lasts for only a few good meals. But a human soul lasts for eternity. We should be equally prepared to plant the seed of the gospel in the heart of lost family and friends. Be prepared.

Perspective

What's It Like to Be Poor?

[Note: The following anecdote was found on the internet in numerous places, with the author unknown. It was also a Facebook post by Dan Asmussen that went viral.]

One day a father of a very wealthy family took his son on a trip to the country with the firm purpose of showing his son how poor people can be. They spent a couple of days and nights on the farm of what would be considered an extremely poor family. As they returned from their trip, the father asked his son, "How was the trip?"

"It was great, Dad."

"Did you see how poor people can be?" the father asked.

"Oh, yeah," said the son.

"So what did you learn from the trip?" asked the father.

The son answered, "I saw that we have one dog and they have four. We have a pool that reaches to the middle of our garden, and they have a creek that has no end. We have imported lanterns in our garden, and they have more stars at night than you can count. Our patio reaches to the front yard, and they have the whole horizon. We have a small piece of land to live on, and they have fields that go beyond our sight. We have servants who serve us, but they serve others. We buy our food, but they grow theirs. We have walls around our property to protect us; they have friends to protect them." With this the boy's father was speechless. Then his son added, "Thanks, Dad, for showing me how poor we are."

Too often, we forget what we have and concentrate on what we don't have. What is one man's worthless object is another's prize possession. It is all a matter of perspective. Makes you wonder what would happen if we all gave thanks for the bounty we have instead of worrying about wanting more. Take joy in all you have, especially your friends.

(https://www.reshareworthy.com/rich-father-poor-family-anecdote/ [accessed 10/16/2019])

> *Oh give thanks to the LORD, call upon His name;*
> *Make known His deeds among the peoples.*
> *Sing to Him, sing praises to Him;*
> *Speak of all His wonders. (Psalm 105:1-2 NASB)*

6

PINE TREES AND PRIORITIES

I sat comfortably in a climbing stand twenty-five feet up a large pine tree not seventy-five yards from where I ended my three-year turkey drought. I figured this particular location had special favor for me since my tree perched on top of a rise, and I could see for miles to the east. The long, brilliant rays of the setting sun illuminated the autumn reds and browns of the deciduous trees in the distance — a glorious sight, ripe for worship and introspection.

The wind blew gently, my tree swayed slightly, and I shivered constantly. Why is it always cold on these late autumn deer hunts? I knew my gorgeous wife and four pretty little daughters were home sitting by the fire waiting for me. The other five children had not yet graced our home. My wife had scolded me for going hunting on two consecutive days. "These little girls need you. You are not home three nights a week already, and now you want to hunt until dark or later two more nights a week. I can't believe you. You need to get your priorities right."

On the other hand, I heard my hunting buddies say, "You can't kill a big buck sitting at the house. You've got to get in the woods."

I wanted to bag a big buck badly. I could see that eight-point, twenty-inch spread over my fireplace. I had a clear vision in my mind, and I determined to go after it.

I also heard the voice of Moses in Deuteronomy 6:4-9:

> *Hear, O Israel: The* LORD *our God, the* LORD *is one. Love the* LORD *your God with all your heart and with all your soul and with all your strength. These commandments that I give you today are to be upon your hearts. Impress them on your children. Talk about them when you sit at home and when you walk along the road, when you lie down and when you get up. Tie them as symbols on your hands and bind them on your foreheads. Write them on the doorframes of your houses and on your gates.*

How could I impress them on my children if I wasn't home when they were? We attended church on Sundays, but my children went to their own class while my wife and I attended our class. On Monday nights, I attended church visitation, which I thoroughly enjoyed because I love to share the gospel. On Wednesday nights, I taught a class and practiced with the church choir while my children were elsewhere. That left four nights a week to be with my girls or to hunt. Oh, my. What's a doctor to do?

There I was, sitting twenty-five feet up in a swaying pine

tree, thinking about God and the beauty of His creation, praying for a big buck to pass by, and trying to push away my wife's voice that kept saying, "You need to get your priorities right."

Nothing ruins a good hunt like your wife telling you the truth and you knowing she's right, even if you don't want to admit it. Why couldn't she have said, "Honey, you go and have a good time, and when you get back, I'll have a steak and potatoes waiting on you. If you get a deer, I'll process it while you eat supper."

Now, wouldn't that make for an amazing hunt? It could happen! But, no. All I heard was "You need to get your priorities right."

Being nagged is like being nibbled to death by little baby ducks. Well, the baby ducks were climbing my tree and chewing on my behind. I was miserable.

Then out of the clear blue, a thought came to me. "You can deer hunt for the rest of your life, but you can't be a daddy to those little girls but for a short time."

Suddenly, I saw my little precious girls all grown up, going to college, and getting married. It frightened me purt near to death. I had much more to teach them and too many hugs and kisses left to give them. An hour of daylight remained, but I worked my way down the tree. Four little girls needed their daddy.

I got home before dark, much to my wife's surprise. "My, you're home early," she said.

"Yes, ma'am, I'm working on getting my priorities right, thanks to you and the Lord."

Don't misunderstand me. Several hours in a deer stand

wasn't wrecking my priorities. The combination of work, church commitments, and deer hunting kept me from my family and frustrated my wife. Something had to give. I later streamlined some of my church commitments after my daughter saw our church's picture on a bulletin, and asked me, "Is this the church where we live?" Ouch!

◆　◆　◆　◆　◆

As I sat in that tree, pondering life, the Lord gave me a useful mnemonic to help me keep my priorities straight. He reminded me I am a Disciple of the Lord Jesus Christ first, a Daddy to my children second, a Doctor third, a Disciple Maker fourth, and a Deer Hunter last. This does not include all my life's activities, but it is a useful tool to keep me straight.

Disciple of the Lord Jesus Christ — This encompasses my personal relationship with Jesus Christ. My personal quiet time each day is a priority I seek to discharge first before any other activity. If the rest of the day falls apart, at least I have spent time with my Master. This ensures that Holy Spirit is part of my life throughout the day.

When I started my journey as a serious disciple of the Lord Jesus Christ, I was in college. I had been a Christian since age eleven, but I wouldn't have called myself a genuine disciple. A disciple is a follower of Jesus Christ who is determined to obey all of Christ's commands, regardless of the consequences. Ponder that a little while, Bro!

Before college, I went to church on Sunday, read a chapter in my Bible every day, but thought little about Jesus or God outside of that. In college, my discipler challenged me to obey God in every respect, submit to Holy Spirit, memorize Scripture, develop a serious daily quiet time, and share the gospel with other college students. I determined to be obedient in all these areas. That's when I found myself on the growth curve in my spiritual journey. Of course, God had to work on many character issues in my life— and still is. I de-double-dog dare you to take the same challenge. Determine in your heart to be a true disciple of Jesus Christ and obey Him in every way, regardless of the consequences — even if He tells you to quit chewing tobacco or listening to country music or to start teaching fifth grade boys in Sunday School. I've never regretted one minute of choosing to follow Jesus as a committed disciple.

A delicate balance exists between ministry responsibilities and family. These two can complement one another or clash. Wisdom and discernment are required to walk that tightrope. Listen to Holy Spirit and to your spouse.

Dad/husband (being husband is first, but Dad fits my alliteration — you get it) — Your wife has only one husband, and your children have only one dad. The opportunity to be their one and only hero should not be squandered. I have male patients who are indiscriminate serial sperm donors without regard to marriage or even serious relationships. They are chronic fornicators and adulterers who pay no attention to the emotional wreckage they leave behind them — and take no responsibility for the children they spawn. They defraud their female companions, making promises they never intend to keep. They are renegade men with hearts of stone.

These men are about as far from what God has called them to be as family shepherds as Jupiter is from the sun. When God captures a man's heart, He turns his heart towards home, towards his wife, and towards his children. "He will turn the hearts of the fathers to their children, and the hearts of the children to their fathers …" (Malachi 4:6). This process is a supernatural transformation that cannot be forced, but you watch and see. When a man gives his heart fully to God, he makes things right with his wife and children.

A God-fearing father is a priest in his home who transfers God's truth from one generation to the next. Psalm 78:5-7 says, "He decreed statutes for Jacob and established the law in Israel, which he commanded our forefathers to teach their children, so the next generation would know them, even the children yet to be born, and they in turn would tell their children. Then they would put their trust in God and would not forget his deeds but would keep his commands."

Brothers, do you realize we get to train our grandchildren even before they are born when we teach our children to trust in God, remember His mighty deeds, and obey His commands? We do this mostly by a way of life teaching. We model righteous living in our daily lifestyle. Who we are and what we do will speak louder and longer than anything we ever say. I'm not minimizing formal instruction, but our walk will travel farther than our talk.

So how do we shepherd our flock?

- We look to the Good Shepherd and follow His example.
- We consider it a privilege and accept the responsibility voluntarily.
- We make it a priority and accept the role eagerly.
- We serve as a model and faithfully represent Christ.
- We meet the needs of our flock in the way God shepherds us (Psalm 23).
- We report to the Chief Shepherd, "and when the Chief Shepherd appears, you will receive the crown of glory that will never fade away" (1 Peter 5:4).

Be the family shepherd and lead them to Jesus at the family altar. Be the priest in your family that openly prays over them and with them. Teach them the Word and model the Christ life for them. Be consistent and be Spirit-controlled. Kids hate hypocrisy.

If we do things right, our children will love the great outdoors and beg us to take them hunting with us. "But, Honey, we're just going to spend some quality time together turkey hunting. We'll be back right before lunch." Now that's a good dad.

Doctor — That's my vocation. Yours may be different, but just as important. Giving priority attention to our vocation is an important part of our testimony. We all should view our workplace as a place of ministry — a mission field. I pray on my way to work that God will make me a life-giving presence at work and give me opportunities to plant the seed of the gospel. Being the best skilled and the hardest working employee or owner is a vital part of our testimony. Performing our work responsibilities "as if unto the Lord" speaks volumes to lost people who tend to do their least to get by. Our work ethic will set us apart and open the door for ministry opportunities.

Disciple maker — David Platt tells the story in his book *Radical* of a young man in Africa who answered David's question, "What do you plan to do with your life?" by saying, "I plan to change the world." David's immediate internal response was to think, "This young man has no school and no training. How will he accomplish this?" With skepticism, he asked him, "How do you propose to do that?" His response: "I plan to make multiplying disciples."

If you think about it, Jesus's disciples were much like that young man in Africa — untrained and uneducated. But as the Pharisees noted, "These men had been with Jesus" (Acts 4:13). That changed everything about them, it changed everything about this young man in Africa, and it can change everything about us. Being with Jesus and being filled with Holy Spirit enables us to do extraordinary things, even change the world by making disciples who will then make other disciples. Jesus's disciples were fisherman, tax-collectors, and political zealots — ordinary men — who changed the world through the disciple-making process.

God convicted me in college that I should pass on to

others the truth I had learned from Him and my mentors. I couldn't escape 2 Timothy 2:2 where Paul said to Timothy, "And the things you have heard me say in the presence of many witnesses, entrust to reliable men who will also be qualified to teach others." Paul discipled his young protégé Timothy. Timothy then taught faithful men who, in turn, taught others. That represents four generations.

Over the years, I have discipled a forklift mechanic, a florist, a power-line repairman, an auto parts shop manager, a truck driver, college students, medical students, an ex-con, an ex-drug addict — all average men who went on to be deacons, Sunday School teachers, better fathers, and, yes, some of them disciple makers. Two of my disciples are pastors, one was a missionary, one leads mission trips full time, and another is an education minister in a church and teaches disciple-making to other churches.

One of the last things Jesus told his disciples before leaving was to "make disciples of all nations" (Matthew 28:19). We call this the Great Commission. We will all have to explain to Him one day our obedience to this command. So, who's your guy?

Deer hunter/turkey hunter — I sometimes feel sorry for myself that I don't have that massive deer mount I visualized for so long. But it requires a lot more sacrifice than I'm willing to make. I gained a vision for children who love Jesus and His church, who love evangelism and missions, who engage the culture on ethical and moral issues, and who will be disciple-makers. That required a significant investment of time and energy on my part. That vision is coming true every day in the lives of my grown children, and it blesses my soul more than an eight-point buck ever could. John wrote, "I have no greater joy than to hear that my children are walking in the truth" (3 John 4).

♦ ♦ ♦ ♦ ♦

I was in a Christian professional businessmen's conference one time when we discussed priorities in a lecture session. I came away from the lecture with a lot to think about. I realize God has the highest claim on my life because He created me from the dust of the earth and breathed into me the breath of life. More than that, He sustains my life every day with His provisions. Finally, He redeemed me from hell, the grave, and the pit by His grace and tender mercy. It makes complete sense that I would order my life around God-given priorities.

In this conference, we were divided into groups of five men with a discussion leader. In our small groups, we were asked to list our top ten priorities, which most of us accomplished rather quickly. We then shared them with the group. I could tell the guys were proud of their spiritual appearing list of priorities.

Then the group leader had us make a second list. This time, he said, "I want you to look at your time and your financial allocations, and then tell us what your priorities really are, not what you would like for us to believe they are."

The entire group groaned. It was a painful experience. A couple of men would not even share their information. One wept out loud. Two more shared with reluctance and some embarrassment. Me? I pretty much had my house in order, thanks to the Lord, my wife, and the pine tree experience.

Let me close with a challenge: Some things in life are more important than others. Our relationship with Jesus Christ is at the top of that list. Family and relatives come next. When my patients become seriously ill, it's interesting to watch how life becomes distilled down to two things: our relationship with God and our relationship with family. Everything else becomes superfluous. It's imperative that we get this straight. Remember: The Bible has a lot to say about being a good husband and a good parent, but zero about being a good turkey hunter.

Make your own two lists of priorities — the one as it should be, and the one as it really is in view of your time and money allocation. Then square them up. Get it straight. If you don't govern your life by your priorities, then someone else will govern your life by their priorities. The writer of Hebrews said, "It is appointed unto man once to die, but after this the judgment" (Hebrews 9:13 KJV). We only get to live once. After that, we must give an account of ourselves to God. Make it count.

If you need a place to think about your priorities, I can point you to a tall pine tree and a climbing stand just off Jerusalem Church Road where you can get your head on straight.

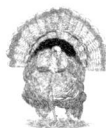

7

LOST

Two friends and I arrived at the property of another friend, "John," for an early morning turkey hunt. The dogwoods were blooming, the grass was covered with dew, and John assured us he had seen and heard lots of turkeys on his farm.

Running right through the middle of his property, the South Pacolet River was swollen due to recent spring rains. The three of us split up so we wouldn't interfere with each other's calling and hunting. Within the first hour, one friend scored a double, taking down two gobblers with one shot not sixty yards across the road from John's house in an open grassy bottom. The other fellow and I had no such success.

I heard turkeys gobble across the Pacolet River, so I had the bright idea to walk one-half mile up the paved road in front of John's house to a bridge over the river to get on the other side of the river, which I accomplished. I had to get on my hands and knees to crawl through briars before reaching open country, but I persevered.

The siren call of gobbling turkeys lured me deeper and

deeper into the woods on the opposite side of the river. The turkeys kept calling and I kept pushing forward into uncharted territory. Suddenly, I found myself in a rain-flooded swamp with dead trees all around. I was up to my knees in swampy waters. Turkeys still gobbled in several directions, but I had lost my direction. I turned about, looking in all directions, and realized that in my turkey frenzy I had wandered far off the beaten path. The hardwoods loomed in the distance behind me, and I stood in the middle of a swamp with dead trees and knee-deep water in every direction.

I saw the sun rising in the east, and I knew if I walked in a ninety-degree angle to the rising sun, I would reach the river. Then, I could follow the river back to the bridge where I had crossed. Confident in my assessment, I thought about turkey hunting a little longer, but decided survival was more important. The closer I got to the river, the deeper the water got and the faster the water flowed. The next thing I knew, I was sloshing through waist-deep cold water with my gun held up at my chest, praying that water moccasins were still in hibernation and reminding myself that gators were a low country thing.

I decided to head diagonally towards where I thought the bridge was so I could stay in shallower water. Fatigue set in, and I couldn't tell if I was any closer to the river.

Notions of spending the night in the swamp flitted through my mind. Despite the cold water from my waist down, I poured sweat with my insulated underwear, camo coat, and turkey vest on because the sun had fully risen on the horizon. The longer I slogged on, the more panic gained control, even though it was broad daylight. For you see, I was lost.

The only thing worse than being lost is being lost and cold. The only thing worse than being lost and cold is being lost and cold and wet, which I was. The only thing worse than being lost and cold and wet is being lost and cold and wet and in the dark. The only thing worse than being lost and cold and wet and in the dark is being lost and cold and wet and in the dark and all alone. The only thing worse than being lost and cold and wet and in the dark and all alone is being lost and cold and wet and in the dark and all alone and hungry. The only thing worse than all of this is no one knowing you were lost.

I pondered what would happen if I couldn't find a familiar landmark before dark. What if I had to spend the night standing in waist-deep, slowly moving water? The prospect frightened me seriously and spurred me on with heart pounding and sweat pouring.

As I pushed my way through deep water and thick under-brush, I found myself walking out of the water up a steep incline — and then abruptly teetering on the precipice of the Pacolet River about ten feet above the water. I threw myself backwards to avoid falling headlong into the water.

My heart pounded. I grabbed a sapling with my left hand. The sapling bent forward, allowing me to lean over the water at a forty-five-degree angle, one hand on my shot gun and one hand on the sapling. I was just before pitching my gun into the river to save myself when I regained my balance and heaved myself backwards onto the riverbank, sucking wind and praising God for all I was worth. Forty minutes later, I was back at my vehicle, exhausted but saved.

Lost. Lost in the woods. What's worse than being lost in the woods? Being lost spiritually without God and without hope. And what's worse than that? Being lost spiritually and not knowing it. Being spiritually lost involves three conditions: being spiritually dead, being spiritually blind, and being spiritually bound. When we are dead, perceiving we are in that condition is difficult. After all, we are dead. When we are blind, we can't see things clearly or at all. We may not even understand our spiritual condition. Let's examine these one at a time:

Spiritually dead — Paul says we were all dead in our trespasses and sins (Ephesians 2:1). Before Jesus imparts His life into us in that born again, life-transforming experience that theologians call regeneration, we are all spiritually dead because of sin. The reason is because "the wages [penalty] of sin is death" (Romans 6:23).

Sin affects everyone, making us spiritually dead. We are all born with a lower nature that loves to sin. We inherit it from our parents who got it from their parents — all the way back to Adam and Eve who committed the original sin. That's why King David said he was conceived in sin (Psalm 51:5), meaning he had a sin nature.

Have you ever noticed you don't have to teach two-year-olds how to rebel against their parents' authority? It comes naturally. That is a child's sin nature coming to the surface. As pretty or handsome as that two-year-old might be, they are already a sinner and spiritually dead in their transgressions and sins.

We are all born spiritually dead. Unless we receive the life of God by receiving Jesus, who is the resurrection and the life, we will stay dead and lost — not in the woods, but in the spiritual realm, which is a much more sinister place.

Spiritually blind — Have you ever talked to somebody about Jesus, and as you were talking, you realized they were not getting it. They were not tracking with you, or worse, they ridiculed you or mocked your belief in Christ.

I once had a seventy-six-year-old patient who was as coarse as a corncob and so profane he hurt my ears and my heart. But somehow, we became friends. He was attached to a thirty-five-year-old woman, who was also my patient. They had a twelve-year-old boy between them. I visited them in their home several times after she had a surgery and a long convalescence. That's how he and I got connected.

Over several years, I explained the gospel to him, but he would always look at me like a calf looking at a new gate. He would turn his head sideways and just stare at me. He didn't get it. He didn't comprehend. "The god of this age [Satan] has blinded the minds of unbelievers, so that they cannot see the light of the gospel of the glory of Christ, who is the image of God" (2 Corinthians 4:4). My patient was blind to the light of the gospel. It wasn't that he lacked intelligence, for he was plenty smart. The enemy of his soul prevented him from seeing the truth. Consequently, this patient and friend of mine was lost in spiritual darkness.

Eventually, my patient required a total knee replacement. I

arrived at the hospital at 6:30 a.m. on the day of his surgery so I could pray over him before the orderlies carted him off to surgery. After I prayed for a successful surgery, I looked up, and this big coarse profane eighty-two-year-old man was weeping. He said, "Doc, I'm eighty-two-years old, and nobody has ever prayed over me like that." I think the Spirit of God was convicting him. Sadly, the orderlies came at that moment and carted him off.

He saw me a time or two after surgery, and he was as mean as ever. One day, I did not have some sample medication for his diabetes that I had previously provided for him free of charge, so he got mad and never came back.

He could see how to drive and move about, but he was spiritually blind. Satan had darkened the eyes of his understanding, so he couldn't see spiritual truth and be saved. He continued to be spiritually lost and spiritually blind.

Spiritually bound — Jesus says, "Everyone who sins is a slave to sin" (John 8:34). For the unsaved person, sin forms a chain that only Jesus can break.

Zeke looked at the floor and shook his head slowly. "I don't think I can do it. I'm addicted and I admit it."

His wife had left him in a storm of anger and hurt when she found out he had been viewing pornography on his home computer for years. More than that, he had been talking to women in online chat rooms and exchanging nude photos. She went ballistic, went to her parents, and wouldn't talk to him for weeks. He was miserable. Nevertheless, he came home from work every day, went to his bedroom, turned on his computer, and returned to his electronic fantasyland. Like a pig returning to the mud, he returned to his sin. He was addicted. He couldn't control himself. He knew it was destroying his marriage, but he couldn't stop. He was in bondage to pornography. Once again, Jesus said, "Everyone who sins is a slave to sin" (John 8:34).

I would like to tell you this story had a good ending, but it did not. Zeke was not a believer. He did not have the power of indwelling Holy Spirit, and he did not comprehend any of the counselling I provided, nor did he have the spiritual power to throw off the shackles imposed by his sinful lifestyle. He never even came close to changing his evil ways. His wife divorced him, leaving him to his electronic fantasy friends.

Pay close attention: Zeke's issue was flagrant and obvious once it was exposed, but all men without Christ are in spiritual bondage to sin. They may not be addicted to porn, drugs, or booze, but they are still in bondage to sin. If you don't believe me, just make up your mind that you are not going to sin for an entire day. After that day is completed, come back and we will resume our discussion.

Even Christians indwelt by Holy Spirit have a difficult time going an entire day without transgressing in some way. We all have a lower nature called the flesh, which loves to sin. How often have we looked at something that was wrong, knew it was wrong, knew it would cause us trouble, knew it would disappoint God, knew it would bring guilt and shame, but we did it anyway and suffered the consequences? How dog-boned dumb was that?

Why would we do this? We do it because we're sinners and addicted to sin. Our lower nature loves to sin. "Prone to wander,

O how I know it. Prone to leave the God I love" ("Come, Thou Fount of Every Blessing," by Robert Robinson).

But that is not the end of the story. Jesus said, "If you hold to my teaching, you are really my disciples. Then you will know the truth, and the truth will set you free" (John 8:31-32). Spiritually bound men can be set free by the truth of the gospel.

I have scores of patients who have been set free from bondage to alcohol, drugs, or sexual bondage by the truth Jesus offers them. Watching as Jesus sets people free from bondage is a wonderful thing. Sometimes, the deliverance is immediate; sometimes, it is over time. Nevertheless, Jesus frees them.

Jesus can give life to a dead man as surely as He raised Lazarus from the dead after he lay in the tomb for four days. Jesus can give eyes that see spiritual truth as surely as He brought light out of darkness at the dawn of creation. Jesus can loose those in bondage to sin as easily as He released the Gadarene demoniac from a legion of demons that held him captive.

To you and me, this may seem difficult or even impossible, but nothing is too difficult for our God. With Him all things are possible, even finding those who are lost in the spiritual realms of darkness. Believe me, for once I was dead but now, I'm alive. Once I was blind but now, I see. Once I was in bondage, but I've been set free — all by the blood of the Lamb. Praise God, I'm free! I can see. I've been found. I'm no longer LOST.

8

PSYCHO TURKEY

My friend Ray called. "Doc, you have any medication for a psycho turkey?"

"A family member?"

"No, Doc, a real live turkey!" he exclaimed.

"What are you talking about?" I asked.

"Well, I've got this tom turkey strutting on the roof of my house every morning. He flies down to our patio to strut for a while. Then, like a psycho, he attacks our sliding glass window repeatedly. We are in our den watching the entire spectacle, but he pays us no attention."

"How long has he been doing this?" I inquired with keen interest, although I am not a turkey psychiatrist. Some of my patients behave like unhinged, wild turkeys, but we won't go there.

"About two weeks since the first of March. We put out bird seed for the songbirds, and then this giant bird shows up and eats all the seed. Then he attacks my glass door. I'm telling you, Doc, he's a psycho."

"Ray, it's not turkey hunting season yet, or I'd come and

put that poor bird out of its misery. I'll come over Saturday morning and look."

Two days later I sat in the den of Ray and Iris Hollifield's home, right near my medical office. We opened the sliding glass door a few inches and sat on the couch to wait. I felt naked without my camouflage. Sure enough, an hour after daylight, we heard scratching on the roof — and it wasn't tiny reindeer. Suddenly, a booming gobble erupted, and all three of us purt near jumped out of our skins. They laughed nervously, and I just smiled like the Cheshire cat in Alice in Wonderland. One more gobble, and a giant bird flew down on Iris and Ray's patio and commenced to pecking at the bird seed strewn all around. He paid us and the house no attention.

"How long will he do that?" I whispered.

"Until the sun gets to the right angle. Then the sliding glass door will begin to reflect his image like a mirror. Watch what happens then."

Tom looked like a twenty-pound gobbler with a ten-inch beard and appeared massive, standing just ten feet from the house. He never looked our way.

I could see the sunshine working its way across the back yard. It reached Mr. Tom, and he became resplendent in all his iridescent glory. He fluffed himself out, warming in the sun, turning one way and then another. The sunshine marched across the patio, finally reaching the side of the house.

Instantly, Mr. Tom stood erect to his full height, eyeing the sliding glass window. He putted twice loudly, then went into a full strut — tail feathers straight up, chest feathers puffed out, head sunk into his chest. His head glowed an intense white, and his engorged caruncles (waddles) flamed fire red. He took mincing steps back and forth across the patio, never relaxing his strutting posture. After about four mesmerizing cycles, he pirouetted and faced the mirror, stalking toward the glass with the tiniest steps, but still in a full strut. We were paralyzed. I was afraid to breath or move, lest I break the spell.

Then lightning fast, he broke strut and threw himself at his opponent in the glass, which he failed to realize was himself. He pecked the window twice in succession. He backed off, turned his head sideways, and stared at himself in the mirror. Turning to the other side, he stared some more. He pulled himself up to his full height and lunged at the glass with his spurs. That psycho turkey attacked the window with his spurs four times in quick succession, each time nearly knocking the sliding glass out of its frame. The attack was ferocious and powerful. After that, I guess he had had enough because he stopped, stalked majestically to the edge of the yard, looked back one time, and slipped into the tree line. Just like that, he was gone.

After observing the ferocity of the attack, I understood why one of my hunting buddies whimpered for a half hour after a big tom flogged him. He thought the turkey was dead, grabbed him around the neck, and held him up for all to see. Well, old tom wasn't as dead as he thought. He flogged my friend with both wings and spurs. My friend tried to hold on while covering his face. He fought the turkey, but the turkey won. Tom flew off, leaving my friend with a lacerated arm. He sat on the ground holding his bleeding arm, staring into space, and whimpering for thirty minutes. It wasn't just from pain or loss of the turkey. He was emotionally traumatized after being flogged by a twenty-plus pound tom turkey. I promise you it was ferocious and powerful.

After catching my breath, I turned to Ray, "That was amazing. He does that every day?"

"Just about every day, Doc. You'd think he would remember the guy in the mirror busted his chops the day before."

"Well, Ray, you have to remember his brain is not any bigger than a pea. I have patients who do the same dumb thing over and over, and their brains are supposedly considerably larger."

Ray just laughed, then got serious and asked, "You aren't talking about me, are you?"

"Ray, if the shoe fits, you will have to wear it."

Then Iris asked, "Is that turkey really crazy, or is that normal behavior?"

I responded, "No, that turkey does not have psychological problems. He is demonstrating normal mating season behavior for a tom turkey. Most gobblers become very competitive during the mating season, just like most teenage boys I know. Thankfully, most members of the human species have learned to be civil in their competitiveness and do not resort to shooting, stabbing, or spurring one another (unless they are intoxicated like some of my patients). When competitors are around, gobblers become aggressive with one another. Your tom attacking his competitor in the mirror is quite normal behavior for a springtime gobbler during mating season."

I thought about that Saturday morning over the years. That

was in the early '80s before everyone had video cameras. If I could have sat in the tree line and videoed that psycho turkey attacking that plate glass window repeatedly, I'm sure I could have easily won $10,000 on America's Funniest Videos some years later. I wonder what if …

♦   ♦   ♦   ♦   ♦

Let's learn some lessons from this demented, forgetful turkey bird:

- He was easily enticed by a small amount of bird food.
- He repeated his same mistakes over and over.
- He didn't seem to learn any lesson at all from his ferocious, physical encounter with the plate glass window. It's a wonder he didn't injure himself or break the window.

Let's discuss all three of these one at a time.

1) A little corn can entice both deer and turkey out of the safety of the woods into the wide-open field. Where I live, feeding deer during deer season is legal, but not turkeys. That is taboo. Now the enemy of our souls knows exactly what entices us. It may be a poker game, a tumbler of vodka, a scantily clad woman, or all three. Who knows? Old Slewfoot knows. He knows what will entice us out into the open. If we put our nose down into that pile, he will put an arrow through our liver before we can jump string. We will bleed out our entire reputation and our testimony.

"Each one is tempted when he is carried away and enticed by his own lust. Then when lust has conceived, it gives birth to sin; and when sin is accomplished, it brings forth death" (James 1:14-15 NASB). This is where LSD is mentioned in the Bible. Lust leads to Sin which brings forth Death. That mnemonic will help us remember the dangerous progression, but remember where it starts: with our own evil desires, our own inordinate (uncontrolled) desires. Then, it leads to sin. That's when we put our face into the corn pile. Death follows: spiritual death, death of our testimony, death of our reputation. The entire process is bloody and ugly. Did I say somewhere that sin makes us stupid and blind?

2) He repeated his same mistakes over and over. Mitch was a big man with a big temper. He was six foot four, 270 pounds, and solid — real solid. He worked all the time, but he stayed angry all the time, mostly over Sandra, his wife, from whom he was separated. She was scared of him. And rightfully so because of his explosive temper and size.

I talked with him and counseled with him a dozen times. I shared the gospel with him over and over, but his response was, "Doc, I know what you are saying. That might be good for you, but I don't really need any of that."

"Mitch, where have you been? I haven't seen you in a year."

Man-mountain Mitch looked sheepishly at the floor and confessed, "Doc, I've been in the slammer for nine months."

"Where? Why?"

"County detention," he responded, still looking down at the floor. Then he looked at me fiercely and unrepentant. "I butt-whipped Sandra's new boyfriend. Showed him who's the boss."

"So he pressed charges?"

"Heck, no. He's still in the hospital, getting surgery on his face and jaw. He's been eating through a straw for eight months. Sandra did, that little …."

"Mitch, how many times have I told you to stay away from that girl? She's no good for you."

"Doc, you don't understand. I love her. I can't stay away from her."

Do you know how many times I've had that same conversation with other patients, both men and women but sometimes with the roles reversed? Sometimes, it is not a person but drugs or booze. When I first started my medical practice, it was video poker. Now, it's internet gambling. Internet pornography is the new cocaine of the internet for both men and boys. Rarely will the internet porn addict admit he keeps going back to the same dumb thing over and over until his wife finds out, and his marriage is ruined. Then he comes to me for help after his hen has flown over the treetops.

King Solomon the Wise tells us that "A prudent man sees evil and hides himself, the naïve [foolish] proceed and pay the penalty" (Proverbs 27:12 NASB). My brothers, are you foolish like that pea-brained turkey that kept doing the same dumb thing over and over, or are you a prudent (wise) man who perceives the danger, the snare laid by the enemy, and hides himself?

3) Mr. Tom didn't learn anything after perceiving his reflection in the mirror and receiving a serious flogging from

the turkey in the mirror. James writes, "Do not merely listen to the word, and so deceive yourselves. Do what it says. Anyone who listens to the word but does not do what it says is like a man who looks at his face in a mirror and, after looking at himself, goes away and immediately forgets what he looks like. But the man who looks intently into the perfect law that gives freedom, and continues to do this, not forgetting what he has heard, but doing it — he will be blessed in what he does" (James 1:22-25).

Now this is a troublesome passage because James the half-brother of Jesus tells us if we don't obey the Word and become doers of it, then we are like that pea-brained turkey that looked at himself in the mirror every day, took a flogging, and then came back for more the next day. How foolish could he be? How foolish can we be?

I think too often we resemble that psycho turkey. How often have we listened to a great sermon on prayer and pledged to God that we would do better? One week later, we forget our promise, and we're watching six-to-nine hours of football every weekend, barely squeezing out ten minutes of prayer a day. We looked at the mirror, walked away, and clean forgot. We deceived ourselves.

How often has the pastor taught us how to study the Bible and challenged us to memorize Scripture? We rally to the cause and promise God we will do better. We even set goals — until deer season comes around. Then, we become forgetful hearers who deceive ourselves. Lord, help us. Already we can't remember what we look like.

But then "the man who looks intently into the perfect law

that gives freedom, and continues to do this, not forgetting what he has heard, but doing it — he will be blessed in what he does" (James 1:25). What does it take to be an effectual doer? It takes two things we discussed in a previous chapter: personal discipline and accountability. By definition, a disciple is a disciplined individual. He disciplines himself to abide in the word and in prayer, and allows himself to be held accountable by a Christian community — the local church. This is what it takes for us to become effectual doers.

When I make recommendations to my patients, sometimes they just plain forget because they have memory issues. Those folks need medication to help them out. However, some of my patients are defiant when I tell them they need to go on a weight loss diet or to quit smoking. I know even as I'm speaking they have no intention of being compliant. There is no medication for them.

If after we hear instructions from God's Word we forget, then "forgetting is disobeying" — as I tell my children. If we are just plain defiant and have no intention of obeying God's Word, then we shouldn't be surprised when a family member rebukes us by saying, "Why do you keep doing that? Are you crazy?"

My brothers, don't forget what you hear. And don't defy what you hear from God's Word. Determine in your heart to be obedient. God's blessings follow those who hear and obey.

(Photo by Kirk Thornton, Unsplash.com)

9

TURKEY DOG

My house is situated on a hill at the end of a quarter-mile long road and in a curve of the Pacolet River. Across the river is 1,500 acres of undeveloped property filled with deer and turkey that love to trespass onto my little forty-acre farm. The river is only forty to sixty yards wide, so it presents no problem for them to cross over.

In March and April, I can stand on the hilltop and hear turkeys gobbling across the river, making me tremble with delight. On one occasion, I heard six turkeys gobbling simultaneously. This caused so much ecstasy that I was caught up in the spirit to the third heaven. Just kidding! Keep your camo shirts on. Enticing them across the water is another thing altogether.

One springtime Saturday morning in April, I attempted to call a gobbler across that wide expanse. I arrived at my predetermined spot, where I had hidden a chair in some tall briars from where I could commandeer the entire river bottom of 200 yards, which was freshly bush hogged and covered with the early morning dew.

As soon as I sat down, got comfortable, and put my head net on, my son's one-year-old chocolate lab, Samson, bounded down the hill behind me. He ran out to my decoy, sniffed disdainfully, and then loped over to lick my camo-covered face. He was a giant, ninety-pound clumsy happy dog.

However, I was not happy and almost lost my religion. "Samson, you big galoot. Who let you out of the garage? Get your big fat behind back to the house." He smiled at me with tongue half out and panted loudly. I gave up. As I stood to haul him back to the house, out of the corner of my eye I spotted a gobbler in full strut 100 yards away to my right. He was already in the middle of the river bottom. Where did he come from? Down I sat. I wasn't going anywhere. Neither was Samson. Fortunately, there was a wall of tall briars between us and the turkey. He couldn't see us, and Samson couldn't see him.

Mr. Tom paraded in all his glory, black as night against the dark green glistening grass of the river bottom. He was glorious and silent. Never once did he gobble in the next two-hour adventure.

Meanwhile, Samson wanted attention. I zeroed in on the gobbler, and Samson kept putting his giant paw on my lap, wanting me to scratch his head. So, with one hand, I rubbed his head or his chin, making him temporarily happy. If I lost concentration while staring at the gobbler, this giant paw would rise and touch my face. "Samson, be still."

Then to my horror, that dumb dog yawned so loudly you could have heard him all the way up to the heavens. His mouth was so wide you could have dropped a Volkswagen into it. Mr. Tom immediately broke strut and stared in our direction.

"Putt, putt." He walked in circles nervously. I clamped Samson's mouth shut. He cried like a baby, so I let him go. He stood up, walked around, and then lay down as if he was going to sleep. *Great, praise the Lord. Finally, some relief.* Then he put his hind leg up on my leg. He wanted me to rub his belly. Oh, good grief. I didn't know whether to cuss or shoot him.

Mr. Tom had spied my decoy and moved fifty yards closer. He strutted again, so I obliged Samson and rubbed his belly. His two-and-a-half-foot long tail flopped up and down rhythmically, so I immediately stopped. He raised his big head and growled at me — a deep-throated growl. I quickly rubbed his belly again — slowly this time. The tail only came up halfway, a suitable compromise.

As the sun topped the hill, it caught Mr. Tom pirouetting on the wet green grass. He was majestic … resplendent … and just out of reach at fifty yards. Then he paraded his resplendent self all the way back to his original spot, one hundred yards away. *Lord, help me!* By now, one hour had passed. I had told Samson "Sit down and be still" a hundred times, and now we were back to square one. I was ready to shoot myself. Forget Samson.

I don't know if God cares about turkey hunting or if He answers my prayers to "Let me kill a big one today." (Don't look so smug. I know you pray the same way. *Lord, please let a big eight-point buck step out into my food plot today. Lord, just let me shoot the biggest buck in the hunt club this year. I promise I'll quit chewing Red Man, and I'll go to church every Sunday for a month.*)

God smiled on me that day. Believe it or not, a Canada goose showed up about that time, fifty yards off to my left, and started honking his fool head off. It was aggravating. I couldn't even hear my sweet, little hen yelp anymore. Well, that set my gobbler off even more than it did me. He stuck his chest out like Foghorn Leghorn, ran toward that goose lickety-split, stopped within forty yards of me, went into a full strut, and gobbled one time. Samson sat up and stared at that gobbler and then at the goose. I put one hand in his collar — lest he bolt after one of them — and one hand on my shotgun, which was really good at thirty yards, but iffy at forty yards. I talked to that gobbler, "Come on, big boy. Ten yards closer, and I'm going to let you meet your maker." That goose honked. Samson growled a low guttural growl, and I prayed. The tension was unbearable. My heart pounded. My hands poured sweat. I breathed with short, panting breaths.

Mr. Tom turned in slow circles at forty yards. His neck was as red as fire and his head glowed white as he eyed my decoy and stared down the goose who still constantly honked. Mr. Tom finally decided to edge closer to Henrietta and, *boom,* he went to turkey heaven. Samson bounded out to stand on top of our prize. He put one big foot on top of the gobbler and looked back at me as if to say, "Look what we did." Shameless.

Well, now I had a turkey dog. True, he nearly pushed me back into my old way of life, but it was an exciting and interesting morning, nonetheless. All Christians have an old man and a new man. We struggle to suppress the old man with his corrupt way of life. We strive to put on the new man. I have to admit Samson was inciting the old man and his sinful tendencies to rise to the surface that day. I'm not prone to lose my temper or to use profanity, but that dog just about got the better of me.

Some of you know what I'm talking about. Certain people or situations trigger your temper and just fly all over you, setting you off. Those people and situations must always be avoided, or they resurrect the old man — which you have diligently put to death every day.

This reminds me of a story of a pastor who bought a lawnmower from a young boy down the street. The next day he couldn't start the mower. He took it back to the young boy and said, "Son, you told me this was a good mower, but I can't get it to crank."

The boy smiled and said, "Preacher, I forgot to tell you. That's an odd mower. You have to cuss it or it won't crank up."

The preacher looked at him sideways and said, "Son, you know I'm a preacher. I gave up cursing a long time ago. I can't even remember how to curse."

The boy smiled again and replied, "Preacher, if you keep pulling on that cord, it'll come back to you."

Well, I tell you, if Samson had cost me that big gobbler, cursing would have come back to me, too — in a big, fat hurry.

When I was in junior high school, a particularly foul-mouthed student was in one of my classes. His mother happened to be our teacher. He was a whiny, recalcitrant, profane young man. She was tall and robust and didn't take any stuff off him. One day, he made the sad mistake of cursing out loud in his mother's fifth period literature class. She quickly left the room, came back in an instant with a large bar of soap, grabbed him by the hair, jerked his skinny butt out of his chair, and stuck that bar of soap deep into his mouth. She put him in a headlock in her rather large, meaty arms and forced that soap bar deeper and deeper into his mouth until it muffled his cries. The classroom was astonished and deathly silent. After a minute, she let him go with a stern warning. He spit soap for half an hour. Not only did he not curse, but his usual constant insolent dialogue also disappeared for weeks. He was three years older and much bigger than the rest of the males in our class, so we laughed up our sleeves for days at his humiliation.

But did soap in his mouth really cure his issue? Not really. His stout mother just intimidated him. He was silent on the outside but still profane on the inside. Jesus castigated the Pharisees for being hypocritical and called them white-washed tombs full of dead men's bones. They pretended to be holy and righteous, but inside they were corrupt.

I have a friend in one of my discipleship groups who works at a place where they have devotionals every morning. He told me he was disappointed with his fellow employees. I asked why. He said, "Doc, they curse and tell dirty jokes right up to devotional time. Then, they stop for the Scripture reading and prayer. Afterwards, they immediately resume the profanity and off-color joking. This leaves my heart broken with their hypocrisy." Would a mouth full of soap help them? Of course not. Jesus said, "For out of the overflow of his heart his mouth speaks" (Luke 6:45b).

In my medical practice, it is not unusual for my patients to be mean, cranky, and sometimes profane. I have a female employee who is as sweet and kind as she can be with glorious red hair. She will point her finger at those patients, call them out, and say to them, "Mr. _____, you need Jesus. This is a Christian practice, and you shouldn't act that way." You know what happens? They straighten up and fly right.

We all need Jesus. He is the only one who can cleanse the inner recesses of our hearts. "The heart is deceitful above all things and beyond cure. Who can understand it?" (Jeremiah 17:9). Only Jesus can transform our hearts. Only Jesus can take away profanity, anger, lust, bitterness, unforgiveness, or whatever flavor of sin is nestled deep in our hearts. My brother, if a lawnmower or a dog or a turkey makes you curse, then you need help. You need Jesus. Call on Him while you can. He always answers.

♦   ♦   ♦   ♦   ♦

Prescription for Bridling the Tongue

(I write prescriptions every day in my medical practice, so let me give you a prescription for bridling the tongue.)

Understand that "no man can tame the tongue. It is a restless evil, full of deadly poison" (James 3:8). Why? Because even Christian men cannot fully eradicate the sin nature embedded in their hearts. How do we go about bridling this "restless evil full of deadly poison" that "is a fire, a world of evil … It corrupts the whole person, sets the whole course of his life on fire, and is itself set on fire by hell" (James 3:6)? Keep reading.

Recognize speech is powerful. Proverbs 18:19-20 says, "An offended brother is more unyielding than a fortified city, and disputes are like the barred gates of a citadel. From the fruit of his mouth a man's stomach is filled; with the harvest from his lips he is satisfied."

Harsh words can offend and break long term relationships that will be harder to restore than breaking down the walls of a castle. At the same time, words can build up, encourage, and edify. Either way, we will eat the harvest of our lips, whether good or bad.

When I was a medical student, a fellow Christian student came to me one day and spoke these unusual words, "Robert, I have spiritual authority to bless and to curse. Today I choose to bless. May the Lord bless you." Then he turned and walked away. I stared after him, pondering what he had said. Those powerful words changed me forever. What he spoke over me was powerfully true. We as Christians do have spiritual authority. We can bless people. The life of God flows through us into the lives of other people through our words. We can verbally impart a blessing to others that can significantly impact their lives. Yet, we so casually throw around those words, "God bless you," with little heartfelt meaning. After the encounter with my medical school friend that day, I have never used the phrase "God bless you" flippantly or casually, because I realize God allows me to impart spiritual grace to others when I speak those words.

But be careful. The converse is also true. We can impart a curse with our angry or profane language as well. "With the tongue we praise our Lord and Father, and with it we curse men, who have been made in God's likeness. Out of the same mouth comes praise and cursing. My brothers, this should not be"

(James 3:9-10). Thoughtfully and intentionally choose to bless.

Whatever captures your mind will eventually capture you. That's why Paul said in Philippians 4:8, "Finally, brothers, whatever is true, whatever is noble, whatever is right, whatever is pure, whatever is lovely, whatever is admirable — if anything is excellent or praiseworthy — think about such things."

Let your mind dwell on these kinds of things. In our culture, filling our minds with corruption is easy, considering what's available on television, the movies, and in popular music. Garbage in, garbage out. The same is true with our minds. No wonder Paul challenged the Colossian church to "Set your minds on things above, not on earthly things" (Colossians 3:2).

I meditated on that verse when I was in college. When I did, the Spirit directed my thoughts immediately to my eight-track suitcase. (Don't laugh. Some of you had eight-track suitcases also.) It was full of rock music eight-tracks, none of which helped me set my mind on things above. I loved my Blood, Sweat, and Tears, and Creedence Clearwater. Still do! But I lugged that suitcase outside and threw the entire thing into a dumpster. With tears in his eyes, my college roommate begged me not to. I said, "No. If it's not good for me, it's not good for you." I began a serious course of Scripture memorization. Whenever I was riding in my car, I worked on memorizing Scripture, setting my mind on things above rather than listening to rock music.

What's in us comes out of us. If our hearts are full of the word of God, Jesus will come out of us — not profanity, anger, or gossip. The best bridle for our tongues is allowing Holy Spirit to control our lives and fill our hearts with the Word of God.

Why not memorize one verse a week for six months? Doing so will transform your life and speech. Be careful though. You might have to throw your eight-tracks away.

Remember, words reflect what is stored in our hearts, especially in moments of passion. Luke 6:45 says, "The good man brings good things out of the good stored up in his heart, and the evil man brings evil things out of the evil stored up in his heart. For out of the overflow of his heart his mouth speaks."

We speak from what is treasured or stored in our hearts. Our heart is like a bank. The experiences of our life put on deposit things both good and bad that will be withdrawn in times of distress. If we deposit corrupt and profane thoughts and language, stay away from the preacher when you hit your thumb with a hammer. If we deposit Scripture and all things "honorable, right, pure, lovely, etc.," then we don't have to be careful who we are around when adversity strikes because the deposit in our bank is Jesus-filled and God-honoring.

King David said in Psalm 19:14, "May the words of my mouth and the meditation of my heart be pleasing in your sight, O LORD, my Rock and my Redeemer."

We should dedicate our hearts and our tongues to God daily. A controlled tongue begins with controlled thoughts. The key to right talk is right thoughts. Right thoughts grow out of a right heart.

So, next time your turkey hunt is purt near ruined by a neighbor's dog, or a coyote, or two lovers out on a stroll (happened to me), shoot the coyote but not the neighbor's dog or the lovers. Remember the lesson of Samson, the turkey dog, and let Holy Spirit control your heart and your tongue so only Jesus-filled words come out. Don't look so skeptical. It could happen!

Samson

◆ ◆ ◆ ◆ ◆

PERSISTENCE

In the 1950s, a family doctor who lived south of Atlanta decided to turkey hunt in Tennessee with several of his friends. His friends left a day early, taking his gear and shotgun with them. Since he was on call for his medical practice, he had to stay up all night. Knowing he was too tired to drive, he decided to take a train.

As he boarded the train, he explained to the conductor how tired he was and insisted he be awakened and put off the train in Chattanooga, no matter how sleepy he might be or how he may protest. Eight hours later, he awoke refreshed, only to find out he had bypassed Chattanooga and was in Knoxville. He stormed off the train, yelling and cursing at the conductor for making him miss his connection with his turkey-hunting friends.

Another conductor remarked, "My, he was really agitated."

The first conductor responded, "Oh, that was nothing. You should have seen the guy I put off at Chattanooga" (as told by my dad to illustrate the power of persistence).

10

DON'T BE SELFISH

It was opening Saturday of turkey season and my first opportunity to hunt. Boy, was I pumped. I had scouted my friend Randy's farm and knew exactly where the birds were roosting. My hunting buddy Harold and I planned to hunt Saturday morning, bright and early.

There was only one hitch: My exceptionally beautiful bride, Carlotta, was two days overdue to deliver our second baby, and I was the obstetrician. (I have delivered eight of our nine children. One was breech, and I had to defer to an ob-gyn on that one.) All week long, I had prayed for her to deliver before Saturday, but God was otherwise occupied. I kept telling my wife, "Saturday is my first chance to hunt. Don't go into labor on Saturday. Don't be selfish." Then we would both laugh, but I was only half kidding. How could she do that to me?

Cell phones had not yet appeared, so all of her girlfriends warned me not to go turkey hunting. They all knew my sinful addiction tendencies. My addictive turkey hunting buddies said, "Pay them no attention. There is no way she will go into labor on Saturday." How would they know?

I devised a foolproof plan. I told my lovely bride, "If you go into labor, just call Randy and have him blow the horn on his truck to alert us, and then we will come on home." My lovely and sympathetic wife agreed to my simple but solid plan.

When Saturday arrived, Harold and I went by our church at 3:00 a.m. to participate in a twenty-four-hour prayer chain, conducted by our church. In retrospect, that was probably a waste of time, at least for me. God might have listened to Harold, but I'm sure He turned a deaf ear to a self-consumed, turkey hunting addicted doctor.

As I walked out the door of my house, my wife had her first labor pain. She said to herself, "Surely not." She almost called me back, but unselfishly let me go. An hour later she was in full blown labor with no way to contact me. By that time, we were prayed up and headed to Randy's place, confident of our opportunity for success that day.

We parked at Randy's and walked a mile downhill into the woods where I had roosted the birds. We set out our decoys, set up in the dark, and waited for daylight. Sure enough, right after daylight, two birds gobbled right away. We smiled at each other in the twilight and called softly. They double gobbled in response. I trembled all over with excitement.

Then I heard a horn blow. I whispered to Harold, "We don't usually hear horns blowing on Saturday morning down here, do we?"

Harold shrugged and replied, "Probably somebody picking up a friend for work."

Then the horn blew again and again. Then it blew constantly. We looked at each other wide-eyed through our camo masks. "Harold, we've got to go!"

"We just got here. The turkeys are gobbling."

"I know, but Carlotta must be in labor, and I'm her doctor. We've got to go."

Harold said a bad word under his breath. Now I knew God hadn't heard his prayers either. We collected our decoys and made our way up the long incline to Randy's house when suddenly we heard a rifle shot, then another, and then another.

"Oh, my goodness, there must be an emergency. We gotta run!"

We took off running for a full mile in multiple layers of cold weather clothing, carrying all of our gear. In short order, Carlotta was headed to labor and delivery, but we were headed to the ICU. We kept stopping to lean on our knees and gasp for breath. I was red-faced and burning up inside all of those layers of clothes. My chest was on fire. Meanwhile, Randy kept firing his rifle into the air. Every time he did so, all I could think about was every kind of obstetrical emergency possible. I'm a doctor. I know all of them. The thoughts spurred me to run faster.

"Come on, Harold. Run faster. It's got to be a terrible emergency."

We finally got to Randy's house and fell on Harold's truck, gasping for breath. Randy was still riding around his horse pasture and firing his rifle up in the air, not knowing we had heard. When he drove up, I gasped, "What? What is the emergency? Is she all right?"

He calmly replied, "Oh, no emergency. She's headed for the hospital. I just didn't know if you heard my horn or not."

Harold and I looked at each other in consternation. I didn't know whether to laugh, cry, or scream. We loaded up in Harold's long-bed Nissan diesel truck that would only travel forty-five mph at maximum speed and set off for the hospital forty-five miles away. I was in torment the entire way. I could see the asphalt going by through the holes in the floorboard of his truck. His truck was so slow I wanted to stick my right leg out and push the truck along faster. That was the longest forty-five minutes of my life.

Finally, we arrived at the hospital. I jumped out of the truck before it stopped, ran up five flights of stairs in full camo — looking like a terrorist — and stood in labor and delivery, looking lost. The head nurse recognized me and pointed toward a room. I ran in and found my wife propped up in the hospital bed, applying lipstick and in no distress whatsoever.

"What's the emergency?"

"There's no emergency, Doctor Jackson. She's progressing nicely. We should have a baby in a couple of hours."

My wife smiled sweetly and asked, "Did you catch a turkey?"

"Bag, bag a turkey. Please say it right."

One hour later, my sweet little Rebecca arrived. I have referred to her as my little turkey baby ever since.

◆　◆　◆　◆　◆

I almost never lived that incident down. At church the next week, my wife's friends clucked like a bunch of hens, "We can't believe you left your wife when she was two days overdue." They shook their heads and clucked like turkey hens in a flock. I hung my head in shame with nothing to say. My turkey hunting addicted friends patted me on the back and whispered soothing words. They all thought my behavior was logical and responsible. My wife never tires of telling that story just to hear her friends tell me how shameful my conduct was.

Now my five grown daughters join in the chorus of clucking hens. "Daddy, how could you? You were so selfish."

I was preaching at a church just last week when one of my wife's longtime friends had to bring that sordid event up to me one more time. Her mother stood beside me, clucking like an old boss hen. I guess I will never live it down.

♦ ♦ ♦ ♦ ♦

In my dictionary beside the word "selfish" is a picture of me, scowling. In your dictionary beside the word "selfish," there is a picture of you. We are all selfish, self-centered, narcissistic guys. We think mostly about ourselves first — what we want and need.

Most of us guys are fairly insensitive. Why is that? We don't spend much time analyzing other people's needs, wants, or feelings. We are pretty self-absorbed. That is why our womenfolk accuse us of being crude, insensitive Neanderthals. We resemble that accusation. How many times has your wife accused you of being selfish and insensitive? "Oh, I don't know,

Doc. How many times has the sun come up since I've been married?" I feel your pain. You know there might be a reason why all of our wives say the same thing about all of us. We're all selfish boors. What's the cure? I'm a doctor, so I specialize in cures. Unfortunately, this cure doesn't come in a pill or a potion. Let me share a scriptural prescription that Paul recommended to the Philippian church:

> *Make my joy complete by being of the same mind, maintaining the same love, united in spirit, intent on one purpose. Do nothing from selfishness or empty conceit, but with humility of mind let each of you regard one another as more important than himself; do not merely look out for your own personal interests, but also for the interests of others. Have this attitude in yourselves which was also in Christ Jesus, who, although He existed in the form of God, did not regard equality with God a thing to be grasped, but emptied Himself, taking the form of a bond-servant, and being made in the likeness of men. Being found in appearance as a man, He humbled Himself by becoming obedient to the point of death, even death on a cross. (Philippians 2:2-8 NASB)*

Now, gentlemen, as Christian men, we know we should "do nothing from selfishness or empty conceit." We know we should, in humility, value others above ourselves. We know we should put the interests of our wives and families above our own interests. We also understand whining and complaining about that expectation is pointless because the next verse describes Jesus' fourfold humiliation as He stepped down from heaven to become man (incarnation). More than that, He became a servant among men. If that were not enough, He became obedient unto death and gave His life for us on the cross. This represents four separate levels of unselfish stepping down in order to put our interests above His own to serve and save us. What an amazing example! What an amazing Savior!

You are saying to yourself, "I could never do that." Oh, yes, you can. Who lives in you as a Christian man? It's none other than Jesus, the very one who set the example and made the sacrifice described in these verses. Paul told us in Colossians 1:27 that it is "Christ in you, the hope of glory." Brothers, Jesus in you and me is our only hope of ever putting to death our selfish lower nature and serving our wives and families as Christ did.

Let me illustrate this with a parable (a fictional story that teaches a biblical message). After eating deep pan pepperoni pizza and drinking chocolate milk, my stomach was a little uneasy. I fell into a fitful sleep and began to dream. In my vision, I was seated by the River Jabbok. No, I was seated onstage at the state turkey calling contest. I was one of ten finalists. The crowd was filled with camo clad turkey hunters, pulling for their favorite turkey caller. No one had ever heard of a medical doctor turkey caller, so no one in the crowd was pulling for me.

Not only that, but there were also only eleven contestants. The number eleven guy had just spit his mouth call out on the stage because he was so full of stage fright. Anyway, I made the cut.

After the first round of calling, I knew I didn't belong with the rest of these guys. Some of the audience actually laughed at my calling. It was humiliating. As I sat on the bleacher with my head in my hands, contemplating dropping out, this guy sat down beside me. "Having a hard day?" I looked up. It was none other than Wayne Kallemup, the three-time national turkey calling champion. He wore cowboy snake boots and the giant silver belt buckle he received for winning the last competition.

I jumped up and pumped his hand. "Man, I'm so honored to meet you. What are you doing here?"

He replied, "I'm a backup judge in case one of these judges couldn't show up or got sick." We had small talk for a few minutes, and then he said, "Looks like you could use some help."

I nodded my head glumly.

He said, "Let me help."

"What? You're going to teach me a turkey call or two? You can't do that. You're a backup judge."

"No," he smiled, "they don't need me any longer. Let's have some fun." He pulled me behind the bleachers, reached up behind my neck, grabbed a big zipper, and pulled it down to my tailbone. He then stepped into my body and pulled up the zipper. I could hear him talking inside of me.

"How did you do that?" I exclaimed in surprise.

"Doesn't matter," he responded. "Now here's the deal. You let me do the calling. It will be you talking and walking, your lips and tongue moving, but me doing the calling. This will be fun."

"Are you sure?"

"Yes, I am sure. Just don't get in my way."

Well, needless to say, I won that state competition, hands down. Those other nine guys didn't know what hit them. Three previous state contest winners were on that stage, and I beat all of them handily, or should I say that Wayne Kallemup beat them handily? For you see, it was him in me that did the calling. Boy, it was fun. You should have seen the faces of those judges. When I — I mean Wayne — started calling in the final round, it was priceless!

Next, I was carried in the spirit to Oklahoma City to the National Wild Turkey Federation annual convention. Thousands of turkey hunters gathered from all over the country. Display booths from all the big-name suppliers and outfitters abounded. I was overcome with joy just to be there. It was like heaven on earth. Before I knew it, I was onstage competing against the best turkey callers from every state. I was so nervous I had the squirts, but I had Wayne with me so I had confidence. I kept saying to myself, "Greater is Wayne in me than all those guys on stage."

Round One was assembly calls and tree calls. I won easily, to the astonishment of the entire crowd. A hush fell over the entire auditorium. I heard one of the judges whisper to another in an Oklahoma drawl, "I declare, he sounds just like Wayne Kallemup."

The other judge responded, "He even smiles and struts like Wayne."

I heard Wayne start to chuckle deep down inside of me.

Then he said, "You're doing good, boy."

We blew through all the early rounds until the final round. I don't know where this came from, but I said to Wayne, "I think I've learned all I can learn from you. I think I can do this next round on my own." I guess I was getting jealous of them talking about Wayne instead of me. I don't know what came over me.

Just like that, Wayne was gone. I could feel the emptiness inside. I called his name, but he was gone. Suddenly, I was all alone, afraid, and insecure. I was no longer confident. I was weak.

They lined the final contestants up on stage. I was the last one. The first four performed superbly to thunderous applause. The judges beamed and wrote down scores. I thought I was going to upchuck on stage. When my turn came, my mouth went dry. I spit my mouth call out on the floor. I heard a 400-pound guy on the front row in a camo shirt, big as a camo blind, guffaw, "He choked." And I did. I choked on the national stage in front of God and everybody without Wayne Kallemup to help me. That little red-neck country doctor didn't belong on the big stage. Now everybody knew it.

I woke up in a sweat with pizza acid in the back of my throat. What an awful nightmare. I found myself saying out loud, "Wayne, come back, come back."

My wife sat up in bed and stared at me, "Who's Wayne?"

I mumbled, embarrassed, "Nobody. Just a bad dream. Go back to sleep."

I hope you are getting the picture by now. Life is way more important than a turkey calling contest, but you do live your life on a big stage with your wife and kids and co-workers as the judges. They constantly watch how you respond to the tough situations in life and the stiff competition. All of us have kids who rebel on occasion. How do you respond? Do you get in the flesh — becoming loud, angry and profane? Or are you a spirit-controlled man who speaks softly with a controlled tongue and wise counsel? What if you do respond poorly? Are you spirit-controlled enough to go back to those you offend to ask forgiveness and set things straight? Have your wife and kids ever heard you say, "I'm sorry. I was wrong. Will you please forgive me?"

You understand that the defining characteristic of a Christian man is what he does with his sin. Not whether or not he sins because we all sin, but what he does with his sin. Does he slough it off and pretend it doesn't matter? Or does he man up, confess, and repent, making things right with those he has offended?

That's what Jesus intended when He said, "Therefore, if you are offering your gift at the altar and there remember that your brother has something against you, leave your gift there in front of the altar. First go and be reconciled to your brother; then come and offer your gift" (Matthew 5:23-24).

Let's land where we took off. We started this chapter talking about selfishness. Jesus submitted Himself to the Father's will and became a servant among men, and ultimately our sacrificial Lamb. What an amazing act of unselfishness. In order to follow in His footsteps, we must put to death the old man with his selfish, fleshly desires everyday so that we can be made alive unto Christ. That is what Jesus meant when telling us to take up our cross daily in order to follow Him. The Christian life is a death-to-self life, a death-to-selfishness life. Only then can we become servants of Jesus Christ and servants of our wives and children. It becomes a lot easier when you are a dead man because a dead man has no wishes, dreams, or desires of his own. He's dead. He's freed up to serve his wife and children and Jesus. It becomes easy to look at your wife and say, "Your wish is mine to obey."

Now, be honest. Does saying that to your wife make you queasy? Does that make your innards rise up in rebellion? It's only because you're not a dead man yet. You need to work on that. Even Jesus had to pray about going to the cross, but He ultimately submitted to His Father's will. He took up His cross, literally, and followed the Father's plan. So must we.

> *Do nothing from selfishness or empty conceit, but with humility of mind let each of you regard one another as more important than himself; do not merely look out for your own personal interests, but also for the interests of others. Have this attitude in yourselves which was also in Christ Jesus, who, although He existed in the form of God, did not regard equality with God a thing to be grasped, but emptied Himself, taking the form of a bond-servant, and being made in the likeness of men. (Philippians 2:3-7 NASB)*

DON'T BE SELFISH!

THE COUNTRY DOCTOR'S TURKEY FEAST

Remove both breasts intact from your recently harvested wild turkey.

Slice one or both breasts into one-inch wide strips (depending upon the number of people to be fed). A turkey breast is quite thick, so I usually slice the strips again into one-inch by one-inch strips.

Marinate the strips for thirty to forty minutes in Paul Newman's Red Wine Vinaigrette.

Apply salt and pepper and seasoning of choice. (I use Butt Rub.)

Cook until done on an electric skillet or in a frying pan.

♦   ♦   ♦   ♦   ♦

Two cans French cut green beans
1 can creamed mushroom soup
½ can dried onions
½ stick of butter

Mix together in casserole dish and cook at 350 degrees for forty minutes.

Add rest of dried onions to top of casserole while in oven five minutes before removing.

♦   ♦   ♦   ♦   ♦

Frozen biscuits cooked in oven at 375 degrees for twenty minutes. Serve hot with butter and jam. (I prefer fig preserves that I have canned myself.)

Who needs dessert when you have biscuits and jam?

I bagged this eighteen-pound gobbler in Woodruff, South Carolina.

11

PUT ON YOUR RUNNING SHOES

In the early 1980s, I, along with one of my hunting buddies and our wives, watched the movie *The Cowboys* (1972) starring John Wayne. Wil Andersen (John Wayne) had to drive a herd of cattle across the Wild West when his drovers abandoned him in search of gold. He settled for a group of schoolboys whom he trained to be cattle drivers. His cook, Jebediah Nightlinger (Roscoe Lee Browne), traveled with them.

At one interesting turn of events when Jebediah was in a hurry to go after the young cowboys, he was propositioned by a lady of the night named Kate (Colleen Dewhurst). In a memorable quote, Jebediah paused, considered his options, pondered his duty, and then responded with a slow baritone voice, "I have the maturity, the inclination, and the where-withal, but, unfortunately, madam, I haven't the time." He left her alone on the prairie as he whirled his horse around and rode quickly away.

My friend and I looked at each other in amazement. I treated patients every day who gave in to the urge of instant gratification and showed up in my office to be treated for STDs, unplanned pregnancies, and broken hearts. But this man valued commitment to friends and duty over instant gratification. I was impressed. Of course, it would have been better if he had been more committed to personal holiness than constrained by a lack of time, but this was Hollywood. All week long, we repeated his statement to each other in our best imitation baritone voices and laughed at each other.

Sometime later, we found ourselves turkey hunting on a friend's property. We pursued a gobbling gobbler that was going away from us until we got discombobulated, another word for lost. We wandered for thirty minutes, looking for moss on the north side of trees. (Isn't that what you are supposed to do?) Finally, we popped out on a logging road, flipped a coin, and turned right. After a turn in the road, we came upon a mobile home.

How do you approach a mobile home in the woods while dressed in full camo and carrying shotguns to ask directions? We laid our guns against the side of the house, took off our head nets, put on big friendly smiles, and knocked on the door at 7:30 a.m. A young lady came to the door dressed in a sheer nightgown. "Ma'am, sorry to bother you. Can you point us in the direction of the main road?"

She smiled broadly, pointed in the direction of the way we were heading, and then said, "You fellows look hot and tired. Do you want to come inside for a glass of tea?"

An awkward silence followed as we averted our eyes and looked at our boots. My friend, in his best Jebediah baritone voice, said, "I have the maturity, the inclination, and the wherewithal, but, unfortunately, madam, I haven't the time."

We looked at each other, exploded into laughter, and fell backwards down the steps. We grabbed our firearms and ran down the road in the direction she had indicated. We heard the mobile home door slam shut so hard the entire house rattled. We kept running lest the homeowner decided to start shooting. We laughed about that incident for a long time.

◆ ◆ ◆ ◆ ◆

One of my pastors used to tell me, "Good intentions will never overcome a bad location." When he said that, I reviewed my life mentally and nodded in affirmation. I had put myself in bad locations all too often and paid the price. Paul told the Roman church to "put on the Lord Jesus Christ, and make no provision for the flesh in regard to its lusts" (Romans 13:14 NASB). If we are serious about walking in righteousness, we have to make plans to keep ourselves out of compromising situations.

I accompanied my pastor Paul Sullivan on church visitation when I was in college. When he knocked on a door, he put his hand on top of the storm door and his foot on the bottom so that if the woman of the house answered the door, she could not open the outside storm door until we ascertained if her husband was home.

Pastor Paul didn't want anybody on the street seeing him or me talking through an open storm door if the neighbors knew the husband was at work. We did our visiting through the door if the husband wasn't home. Doing so protected our reputation and avoided temptation. It also kept us from being in a bad location. Pastor Paul once said he knew pastors who said they could visit women in their homes all alone without being tempted. His response? "I wonder what else they would lie to me about."

You remember Joseph, don't you? Joseph was the number one man in Potiphar's house. Potiphar's young and attractive wife took a shine to the young and handsome Hebrew steward and began to entice him every day when the boss man was away. Joseph made his position clear.

But he refused. "With me in charge," he told her, "my master does not concern himself with anything in the house; everything he owns he has entrusted to my care. No one is greater in this house than I am. My master has withheld nothing from me except you, because you are his wife. How then could I do such a wicked thing and sin against God?" And though she spoke to Joseph day after day, he refused to go to bed with her or even be with her.

One day he went into the house to attend to his duties, and none of the household servants was inside. She caught him by his cloak and said, "Come to bed with me!" But he left his cloak in her hand and ran out of the house (Genesis 39:8-11).

Joseph put his running shoes on and got out of there. He didn't debate or dialogue with her. Rather, he ran for the hills, protecting his integrity. He knew his good intentions were no match for that bad location or that evil woman.

Joseph was still placed in prison, due to the duplicity of

Potiphar's wife, but this was part of God's plan to eventually elevate Joseph to the second place in the kingdom. He had to go through prison to get to the palace. This is a great example of Isaiah 55:9 and illustrates God's sovereignty over our lives, even when it is difficult to understand.

Joseph maintained his integrity, protected his honor, and preserved for himself the opportunity for future service by fleeing from temptation. Paul advised Timothy to do the same: "Flee the evil desires of youth, and pursue righteousness, faith, love and peace, along with those who call on the Lord out of a pure heart" (2 Timothy 2:22). In other words, put on your running shoes and flee from a bad location.

I sat at the lunch table in my office one day when a pharmaceutical rep shared with me and my partners one of his experiences:

> I was at Myrtle Beach at a medical conference. After a long day, I went out to supper with my fellow drug reps. After supper, one of the reps said, "I know a great topless bar not far from here. Let's go." My heart sank, but I didn't have the courage to say "No." We all loaded up in a cab and started off with the other guys, laughing and talking. I was so sick I thought I would vomit. I'm a Christian. I had no business going there. What if my wife found out? Jesus would already know. We came to a stop light, and I suddenly opened the cab door and lurched out

onto the sidewalk breathing heavily. The other guys said, "Are you all right? Where are you going?" I responded, "I'm a Christian. I've got no business going to a topless bar. It would ruin my testimony." The guy in the middle in the back seat said, "Me, too. I'm not going either." The third guy in the back seat said, "Well, if you're not going, neither am I." The first guy who initiated the invitation cursed and said, "Well, _____, if you're not going, then neither am I." Then I said, "There's a new Star Wars movie on. Let's go see that." And that's what we did, and we had a good time.

Now that brother was a little slow on the pickup, but he got his running shoes on. James says, "Whoever turns a sinner from the error of his way will save him from death and cover over a multitude of sin" (James 5:20). Who knows how much sin that brother prevented that night by getting out of the cab and saying, "Guys, I'm a Christian. I've got no business going to a topless bar." An honest confession, coupled with running shoes, improved his testimony and his position immediately.

I can hear some of you saying, "Doc, I appreciate your suggestions, but you don't have to worry about me. I've got my guard up." I'm pretty sure that's what King David thought just before he peeked through the lattice on the rooftop and spied Bathsheba taking a shower. He was the man after God's own heart. He was the psalm writer of Israel. He knew how to worship God. After all, he wrote praise and worship songs. He thought he was immune to temptation. He thought he had a hedge of protection around himself.

David's confidence bordered on arrogance, which led to pride. Pride always tells God, "My way is better than your way." David chose his way — the way of adultery, conspiracy, and murder. Royalty sins in the same ugly way as the common folk do. Paul gave some good advice to the Galatian church in Galatians 6:1, "Brothers [and sisters], if someone is caught in a sin, you who are spiritual should restore him gently. But watch yourself, or you also may be tempted." Did you catch the last phrase? "Watch yourself, or you also may be tempted."

Here's my question: What if you were turkey hunting and lost in the woods, but you were all alone? What if you had knocked on the door and a scantily clad fair maiden came to the door and invited you in to a tea party? What would you do? Would you open the door of the cab and get out? Would you put on your running shoes and flee youthful temptation? Would you put on your best Jebediah Nightlinger imitation and say, "I have the maturity, the inclination, and the wherewithal, but, unfortunately, madam, I haven't the time" — and then politely excuse yourself. You better decide in advance what you will do. It's always best to know where the fire escape is before the fire starts.

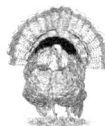

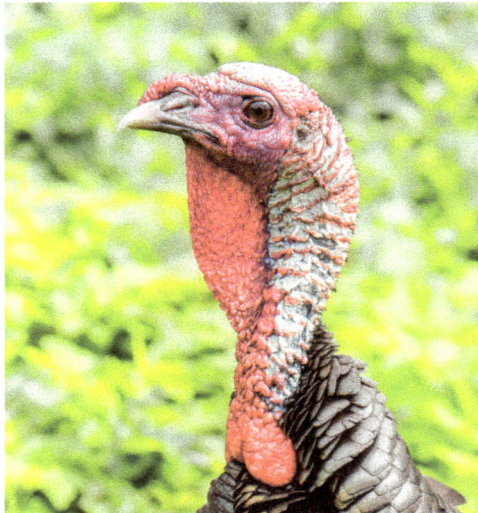

(Photo by Dulcey Lima, Unsplash.com)

12

Live Their Entire Lives Without Ever

"**D**oc, what you are seeing from this vantage point is a thousand acres of the best hunting in South Carolina." The hunt club manager showed me property that had just come available to create a hunt club.

"The entire club is 3,000 acres, bordered on one side by the river you can see there and on two sides by an impenetrable swamp. A paper company whose CEO opposed hunting owned the land. The owner paid a man to patrol the fence on the fourth property line every day for forty years to keep poachers off. She is now gone to wherever PETA folks go to get their rewards," he said with a sarcastic snort.

"Where's that, you reckon?" I asked.

"I'm pretty sure they have to spend eternity serving tables at Texas Roadhouse," he responded with a guffaw, slapping his knee so hard the birds flew out of the trees. He took a minute to compose himself.

"These woods have only been logged twice in the last forty years: twice for pines and once for hardwoods. There are logging roads aplenty, so most of the property is accessible. One-hundred-year-old mature oak trees are everywhere. This place is amazing. Multiple streams flow all year and empty into the river. Plus, there are two natural ponds with at least five acres each.

"The deer and turkey population exceed that of any hunt club I have ever managed. Last fall, I counted six flocks of thirty turkeys in one day. Herds of twenty deer are common. Plenty of mature bucks live in these woods. I apologize that I don't have any pictures yet. Doc, there are deer and turkey here that have lived and died without ever seeing the face of a man." He turned and stared at me to let that sink in. "There are turkey and deer in there that have never been hunted in their entire lives or the lives of their forebears."

As I drove home that day, I pondered the possibilities of hunting in such a place and tried not to drool on myself. However, the membership price was too rich for my blood, and the club rules didn't allow anyone to take guests. At that time in my life, I was teaching my sons how to hunt. Such a hunt club would have been no good to me.

◆　◆　◆　◆　◆

Fast forward a number of years. I'm standing on the top floor of a high-rise motel in Delhi, India, speaking to a missionary friend raised in India and looking through a large plate-glass window at the city. We could see homes and businesses for miles through the early morning smog.

"Doctor, we can only see a small portion of the city from here, but 29 million people live in Delhi. About 1.2 billion people live in all of India. One out of every seven people in the world live in India. Most of them are Hindus, some are Muslim, and some are Buddhist. Less than 0.5 percent are Christians. Many legal and cultural obstacles prohibit sharing the good news of the gospel here in India."

"Most people in India will live and die without ever hearing about Jesus. People here have lived and died for generations without ever hearing the gospel." He turned and stared at me to let that sink in. The tears rolled down both sides of his face as he said, "These are my people. I love them dearly. I would give my life for them to come to Jesus." Turning back to the window and weeping, he whispered, "O Jerusalem, Jerusalem, you who kill the prophets and stone those sent to you, how often I have longed to gather your children together, as a hen gathers her chicks under her wings, but you were not willing" (Matthew 23:37).

I can't tell you how moved I was to hear him whisper the very words of Jesus, the cry of the Master's heart as He wept over the city that would soon reject Him as they had rejected all the prophets before Him. My missionary friend was broken-hearted over the lostness of his people and desperate for them to know the Savior who could deliver them from sin and darkness. That top-floor encounter in Delhi affected me greatly.

According to ReachBeyond.org, over 2 billion people on planet earth have never heard a clear presentation of the gospel (https://reachbeyond.org/Advocate/RBActionGuide.

pdf, accessed October 30, 2019). Missiologists of the Joshua Project initiative say 7,000 people groups representing 42 percent of earth's population are unreached, which means less than 2 percent of these people groups are Christ followers, and less than 5 percent call themselves Christians (https://joshua-project.net/resources/articles/has_everyone_heard, accessed October 30, 2019).

Following are some sobering facts about the fifty largest unreached people groups:

"All of these people groups have less than 2 percent who are Christ followers. Individuals in these groups have very limited, if any, access to the gospel. These groups are comprised of 1.48 billion souls. One in five people on earth live in these fifty groups. Every group is larger than 10 million in population. None have an indigenous church capable of taking the gospel to the entire group. These groups are predominantly Muslim, Hindu, and Buddhist" (https://joshuaproject.net/resources/articles/has_everyone_heard accessed August 11, 2019).

That doesn't mean the remaining 5 billion people on earth are Christians; it just means they have had the opportunity to hear and believe or reject the gospel. That's why Jesus said, "For wide is the gate and broad is the road that leads to destruction, and many enter through it. But small is the gate and narrow the road that leads to life, and only a few find it" (Matthew 7:13-14).

You can gather from my turkey hunting stories that I am an avid turkey hunter, but that is not my real passion in life. My real passion is telling people about Jesus and what He can do for them. That is why I wrote my second book, *The Family Doctor Speaks: The Truth About Seed Planting — Equipping Believers for Evangelism*, in which I describe my many opportunities of sharing the gospel with friends, family, and patients locally and around the world on mission trips. The book is designed to train and equip other believers to be better at planting the seed of the gospel.

Bagging a big tom lights my fire, and I brag about it for weeks and tell about it for years. But what really gets me excited is seeing somebody come to know Jesus. My genuine passion in life is planting the seed of the gospel, both here in my local circle of influence and overseas to the ends of the earth. I came to an understanding a long time ago that real joy in the Christian life is a by-product of obedience to the commands of God, outlined in Scripture. The more I obey, the more I experience joy on my Christian journey. Isn't that what we sing in church? "Trust and obey for there's no other way to be happy in Jesus but to trust and obey" ("Trust and Obey" by John H. Sammis).

Now, there's a bug-a-boo in our culture I call selective obedience, which is nothing more than disobedience. What that means is we choose certain culturally acceptable commands in Scripture to obey. Those that are personally or culturally difficult, we neglect or disobey. Let me illustrate with a personal experience.

When I was first married, I learned grocery shopping with my wife was entirely different from my style of shopping. My style was like a Navy Seal surgical strike: in and out, in the dark, and so fast nobody knew I was there except by the receipt I left behind at the register. *Wham, bam,* I got the Spam!

Agreeing to grocery shop with my new bride after the honeymoon was a hard lesson. I slipped on my black Ninja suit and my night vision goggles and was ready to execute the mission, until I realized that, to her, going to the grocery store was an experience and a social event. She sauntered down every aisle, examining each article and comparing prices. She spoke to people she didn't know, as if they were long lost friends. I was beside myself with existential angst.

When we approached the vegetable counter and she casually instructed me to "select a head of lettuce," I grabbed one off the shelf with a deft, swift motion and deposited it in the cart without any wasted motion. My lovely new bride screeched in front of God and everybody and almost went into a convulsion: "No, no, you can't do that."

She jerked that head of lettuce out of the cart, put it back on the shelf, and began to carefully examine every head of lettuce before selecting one and putting it in the basket. "That's how it's done." I had no idea. My mama never told me. Every woman in the store was shaking their head sadly. I was mortified. I could have fallen through the floor.

After my wife moved on, I went to the lettuce shelf and began to heft them up one at a time. They were all the same. I looked at my wife in amazement but had the early marriage wisdom to say nothing in public. I've kept it to myself all these years until now. Oh, Lord, I feel so much better just getting that off my chest. I knew you brothers would understand.

Now here's the point. We Christians who call ourselves disciples — people who will make other disciples and teach them to obey all things that He has commanded us — well, I hate to break it to you, but we are just like women at the vegetable counter at the local store who pick some and leave the rest. We are just as selective as they are when it comes to obeying God. Selective obedience is disobedience. We choose to obey that which is easy or culturally acceptable, and we put the rest back on the shelf, but get this — they all weigh the same. They are all the commands of Almighty God. Joy and fruitfulness come from complete obedience.

Jesus told His disciples, "I have told you this so that my joy may be in you and that your joy may be complete" (John 15:11). What was it He told them that would make their joy complete? In the previous verse, He said, "If you obey my commands, you will remain in my love, just as I have obeyed my Father's commands and remain in His love" (John 15:10). Obedience leads to a close relationship with Jesus, which in turn leads to complete joy. If you lack joy in your Christian life, then you need to examine the full extent of your obedience to God's commands. Disobedience always detracts from your joy.

The consequences of obedience in America are different from that in Hindu India or Muslim Middle East. In those places, taking the name of Christ and obeying His commands often means being ostracized from your family, losing family inheritance, losing employment, losing friendships, and sometimes enduring death threats. New believers often have to move away to another city or another country to find employment or safety from persecution.

Knowing this, what Jesus told Nicodemus makes sense,

"No one can see the kingdom of God unless he is born again." Nicodemus's response makes better sense from a Pharisaical cultural perspective, "How can a man be born when he is old?" Nicodemus asked, "Surely he cannot enter a second time into his mother's womb to be born."

Nick knew if he followed Jesus he would be ridiculed and would lose his Pharisee friends, his privileged position, and possibly his financial holdings. He might even be physically abused despite his lofty position. His family would reject him. He would have to start all over in life — like being born again. How could he do that when he was so old? It would be as difficult … nay, as impossible … as entering into his mother's womb again. Nicodemus understood clearly what Jesus asked him to do.

For us in America, obedience is a decision with far less consequences (at least for most of us at this time). The challenge for us is to choose to be fully, not selectively, obedient to our King. To our brothers and sisters in Hindu and Muslim countries, doing so is a life or death decision. It's starting all over … being born again both spiritually and in every other way in life. For them, it is taking up a cross, an instrument of death, not the troubles of life to which we typically think the cross refers. It entails following Jesus even if it means loss of family, employment, or life.

Dietrich Bonhoeffer chose to follow the cross in Nazi Germany where obedience to Christ led to imprisonment and ultimately death. He once said, "Only he who believes is obedient, and only he who is obedient believes." He also said,

"One act of obedience is worth a hundred sermons" (inspiringquotes.us/author/9534-dietrich-bonhoeffer, accessed October 21, 2019).

So what holds us back from being fully obedient? In my discussions with men over the years, I have discovered three main things hold them back: fear, sin, and a lack of faith.

Number one — fear. Men often fear what other people will think of them if they give themselves fully to obeying God. They fear being labeled a fanatic for Jesus. Listen, brothers, a fanatic is just someone who loves Jesus more than you do and no longer cares what people think about him. He only cares what God thinks about him. Understand clearly that God is our primary audience, and it is before Him we must stand and to whom we must give account. "Fear of man will prove to be a snare" (Proverbs 29:25). "The fear of the LORD is the beginning of wisdom" (Proverbs 9:10).

Sometimes, men fear God. They are afraid that if they give themselves to fully obey God, He will make them go to Africa, live in a grass hut and eat bugs for the rest of their lives. Brothers, the happiest place in the world is in the center of God's will — even if you have to eat bugs! Obey God and He will make your joy complete. "Perfect love drives out fear" (1 John 4:18). He loves us with a perfect love, and we should never fear a God like that who has our best interests at heart.

Number two — sin. Some men will not fully obey God because they love their sin more than God. Sometimes it is a sinful habit. Sometimes it is a sinful relationship. Either way, the sin becomes an idol in their lives and supplants God as king in their lives, stealing their joy and fruitfulness in God's kingdom.

Unconfessed sin of any kind short circuits the vast power of God in our lives. The only cure is to repent and confess that sin and choose to obey God in every area of life. It boils down to a decision that has to be made in a sinner's heart, fostered and fortified by Holy Spirit over time to help us keep this commitment. It is easy for me to say, but it is hard for any man to do. If you are embroiled in a life of sin, deciding to do right may sound impossible. But trust me, it is not. I know many a man who has repented of sin and chosen a life of obedience to God.

Number three — lack of faith. Lack of faith means an unwillingness to trust God to keep His promises. None of us would admit that publicly, but our actions prove it. God has called us, yea, commanded us to do all manner of things that we fail to do because we don't trust Him to uphold His end of the bargain.

For example, many Christian men I know do not even come close to giving a tithe of their income to God because they don't trust God's promise when He says, "Give, and it will be given to you. A good measure, pressed down, shaken together and running over, will be poured into your lap" (Luke 6:38a). Either God is a truth teller or a liar. Make up your mind. In Malachi, God challenges us to test Him because He is so confident He can uphold His end of the bargain.

What about sharing the gospel? God promised He would be with us to the ends of the earth as we go about making disciples of all the nations, yet we make tons of excuses not to be personally involved with evangelism here or overseas. There is a theological term for that — bologna! It's just a pure lack of faith that God will honor your efforts at seed planting and open doors for you to be involved with overseas missions. Practice saying this with me: "Here am I, Lord. Send me." Just wait and see what God does with your faithful obedience.

What about praying? "If you abide in Me, and My words abide in you, ask whatever you wish, and it shall be done for you" (John 15:7 NASB). Now either Jesus was speaking truth or not. Make up your mind. If you fulfill the conditions, abiding in Jesus and His word, what is to keep you from being the all-time greatest prayer warrior ever? Oh, I see. You don't believe He will answer your prayers for some ill-defined reason. Oh, ye of little faith. Why not? Your sins have been washed in the blood. You are full of the Holy Ghost. Your name is in the Lamb's book of life. You are a citizen of heaven. You have been given access to the very throne room of God! Jesus is the one who said whatever you ask it will be done for you. Screw your faith to the sticking place and ask God for big, bold things.

♦ ♦ ♦ ♦ ♦

I pray often that God will show me if there is any area of my life where I'm not being fully obedient to Him or His word. I have this persistent dread I will awaken one day and realize

I have been blinded by the American culture or the American church way of doing things and that I have missed obeying God fully in some critical area of my life. I don't want to get to heaven and realize I had cultural blind spots keeping me from obeying God.

Can I encourage you to speak to God along the same lines, asking Him to reveal any areas of disobedience or blind spots in your life? Purpose in your heart to be fully obedient to God and His word. Only then will your joy be made complete.

Why do I make such a big deal about all this? Because there are 1.2 billion people who have lived their entire lives without ever hearing about Jesus and who are waiting for guys like you and me to obey Jesus' command to "Go and make disciples of all the nations." What are you waiting on?

13

INTEGRITY

Some years ago, two little piebald does showed up on my farm. They looked like little goats because they had so much white coloration. I enjoyed standing on my upstairs porch at night and shining spotlights on them during the off season. Their white colors made them stand out like a beacon. I caught a good picture of them on a game camera that I still keep in my wallet. I grew fond of them over a three-year period of time.

However, after those three years I decided I would harvest them the next deer season before someone else did to collect their hides, which would make unique rugs or wall hangings. I calculated that if I let them live much longer, they would die by another hunter or by a vehicle collision. We watched them all summer. My friends kept saying to me, "You better go ahead and take those deer or somebody else will." I would respond, "It's not deer season. I'll just have to wait." Even some of my family members warned me, "If you wait too long, you're going to lose those piebalds." Again, I said, "No, it's not deer season. I'll just have to wait."

Well, you guessed it. They disappeared before the season opened. We never saw them again. I don't know if a coyote or a poacher got them, or if they died from a vehicle collision. Nevertheless, I didn't get them! I still miss those pretty little deer, and I still wish I had those hides. I'll show you the picture sometime.

This wasn't the only time I've been tempted to fudge on the game laws. I was showing a friend around my property one time, and I showed him where we planted food plots and put out corn for the deer.

He commented, "I don't see any corn."

I responded, "It's turkey season next week. The DNR doesn't allow any corn on the ground two weeks before turkey season."

He looked at me incredulously, "How long have you lived here?"

"Twenty-two years," I said.

"Has a DNR agent ever visited your farm?" he asked.

"No, sir."

"Well, then, what does it matter. Feed those turkeys. They'll never know."

"You may be right, but I'll know. My sons and sons-in-law will know, and God will know. I don't break the DNR rules even when no one knows."

He looked at me in surprise and shrugged his shoulders. Our conversation revealed a lot about him. For you see, the real test of a man's character is what he does when no one is looking. Hunters are often all alone in the woods, far away from prying eyes, just them and God. Integrity counts with hunters.

Jesus said, "He who is faithful in a very little thing is faithful also in much; and he who is unrighteous in a very little thing is unrighteous also in much" (Luke 16:10 NASB). If we can't be trusted to abide by DNR rules in the middle of nowhere, we can't be trusted anywhere.

I was hunting in Union, South Carolina, with my good friend Karmen when I called up a gobbler right on the property line. I sat next to a big oak along the barbed wire fence and commenced to calling him. Well, if that old long beard didn't fly down on the neighbor's pasture about forty yards out. This little black turkey on my left shoulder immediately said, "Shoot him. No one will know. You can scoot under the barb wire and throw him over on this side."

A little white turkey on my right shoulder responded, "Don't do that. You'll be trespassing and your conscience will bother you." The black turkey said, "Come on. No one will ever know." The white turkey whispered, "You will know, and God will know."

The gobbler pranced to within thirty yards and gobbled so loud that the whole woods shook. I understood once again that life is not fair. Frustration flowed over me like a fever in hot summer. I itched all over and poured sweat. I thought I was developing hives. Foolishly, I raised my gun to look at him over my sights. Thirty yards! Easy-peasy! Lemon-squeezy! In the freezy!

I shook my head and lowered my gun to my lap; then, suddenly an ATV rounded the corner, spooking the gobbler and causing him to fly away. It spooked the *bejeebers* out of me, too. It was the landowner and another man riding the fence line and talking out loud. They never saw me and went right on by, totally unaware of my presence. What if I had shot that bird and crawled under that fence? I would have been caught red-handed, bird in hand, pants down. Couldn't you see the headlines: "Spartanburg Family Doctor Arrested for Trespassing," or, "Spartanburg Family Doctor/Deacon/Sunday School Teacher Arrested for Trespassing"? Oh, my!

The Bible says, "Food gained by fraud tastes sweet to a man, but he ends up with a mouth full of gravel" (Proverbs 20:17). Well, I'm here to tell you that poached turkey eaten in secret will break your teeth on number 4 shot! You could also lose your gun and your license and end up in the slammer. Don't listen to the black turkey. Be faithful even in the little things. My wife always tells my kids, "If you lie, you'll cheat. If you'll cheat, you'll steal. If you'll steal, you'll kill." It's a natural progression from the little things to much bigger things. That's why the little things are so important.

What does it mean to have integrity in the little things? What exactly are the little things?

In what a man says — A man of integrity keeps his promises. He says what he means and means what he says. His word is his bond. If he says he'll do something, then you can forget about it. You don't have to bird-dog him because he will get it done.

A man of integrity speaks the truth even to his own hurt. He doesn't shade the truth or hide the truth. He speaks the full truth. More than that, he speaks up when the truth is unpopular because he defends the truth and promotes the truth. He is a truth speaker.

Psalm 15 says:

> LORD, *who may dwell in your sanctuary? Who may live on your holy hill? He whose walk is blameless, and who does what is righteous, who speaks the truth from his heart; and has no slander on his tongue, who does his neighbor no wrong, and casts no slur on his fellowman, who despises a vile man but honors those who fear the* LORD; *who keeps his oath even when it hurts, who lends his money without usury and does not accept a bribe against the innocent. He who does these things will never be shaken.*

Jesus said, "Every idle word that men shall speak, they shall give account thereof in the day of judgment" (Matthew 12:36 KJV). Integrity in what we speak is a serious issue.

In what a man sees — "The eye is the lamp of the body. If your eyes are good, your whole body will be full of light. But if your eyes are bad, your whole body will be full of darkness. If then the light within you is darkness, how great is that darkness" (Matthew 6:22-23).

Guarding our eyes is the same as guarding our hearts. The eye is the gateway to our hearts. Sadly, we live in a corrupt, pornographic world, flooded with fleshly images on television, movies, and cell phones.

When I was young, a man had to go find pornography.

Today, porn pursues a man and young boys, especially through handheld devices. If we are not committed to personal integrity with our eyes, we are going to be snared by fleshly images and become addicted. Addiction to porn ruins a man's spiritual life and family life. It creates constant shame and spiritual impotence. The porn-addicted Christian man has no spiritual power or spiritual authority. His dark secret causes him to become side-lined and paralyzed.

Porn addiction is so prevalent (60 percent of Christian men admit to issues with porn) that there are counselors I refer people to who specialize in counselling men addicted to pornography. If you are one of these men, purchase and watch The Conquer Series — The Battle Plan for Purity by Kingdomworks Studios. I strongly encourage you to watch this with other Christian men who are strongly committed to personal purity. I also recommend visiting the website, setting-captivesfree.com. "If then the light within you is darkness, how great is that darkness" (Matthew 6:22).

In what a man thinks — "As a man thinks in his heart, so is he" (Proverbs 23:7 KJV). Right thoughts determine right attitudes, and right attitudes produce right actions. That's why Jesus warned us that "anyone who looks at a woman lustfully has already committed adultery with her in his heart" (Matthew 5:28).

Sin begins with our thought life. Jesus immediately went on to tell His audience, "If your right hand causes you to sin, cut it off and throw it away. It is better for you to lose one part of your body than for your whole body to go into hell" (Matthew 5:30).

Was He advocating self-mutilation? No. He taught that we should amputate those dangerous thoughts immediately before they poison our thought life and then lead us to adulterous activity. Like I've told you before, sin makes us stupid and blind. Sane and intelligent people don't do the dumb stuff they do until they have allowed sinful thoughts to seep into their hearts, affecting their good judgment. Then, they become stupid and blind.

I once counselled with a businessman's wife who was both brokenhearted and furious. Her husband, who claimed to be a Christian man, was openly flirting with a female employee, despite his wife's confronting him. His other female employees quit their jobs in disgust over his sexually explicit conduct in the workplace. His wife made such a stink that he fired the female employee, but then placed her as a manager of another business he operated in town.

When his wife found out, she started divorce proceedings, especially after he left the family on Christmas Day to go visit the other woman. What surprised me was that in the midst of adultery and divorce proceedings, he had the audacity to go on a mission trip with his church. I prayed the entire week that the Spirit of God would convict him of his sin, but I suspect he was too stupid and blind.

That businessman didn't wake up one day and say to himself, "I'm going to ruin my reputation and wreck my family." No, his sin started with a thought … with watching that female employee sashay down the hall at his workplace and wondering to himself, "I wonder what it would be like …" He didn't have the integrity to amputate that thought like a gangrenous big toe on a diabetic foot. It takes swift and decisive action like a surgeon with a scalpel. Jesus said, "Cut it off and throw it away." Now he is divorced, his kids won't talk to him, and his Christian testimony is ruined.

Are you a man of integrity? Can you be trusted to do the right thing always, even when you are all alone and no one is watching except God? We can pretend to be men of integrity when others are watching, but genuine integrity manifests itself when we are all alone. Integrity in our actions is the fruit of the tree. The root of that tree is buried in our hearts. That is why the wisdom writer said, "Above all else, guard your heart, for it is the wellspring of life" (Proverbs 4:23).

(Photo of a piebald deer taken with game camera on the Jackson Farm – our home.)

14

A Dog in the Hunt

One Saturday morning when I was sixteen, my dad woke me early and said, "Come on, boy, we're going quail hunting."

"But I'm still sleeping," I mumbled.

"You can sleep when you get to heaven."

I thought about that for a microsecond, then responded, "There ain't no sleeping in heaven. The lights are always on."

Dad was dressed in brush pants and a camo shirt and was walking down the hall towards the kitchen. He responded over his receding shoulder, "Well, you can find out when you get there. Get dressed."

My dad was a doctor, an ex-Vietnam vet, a major in the Air National Guard, and no nonsense. I got dressed quickly.

We arrived at my Uncle Scott's farm to find several horses saddled and two dogs barking. My uncle was proud of his national field trial champion bird dogs. They were stout and muscular and could run all day. This November morning was cold and crisp with crystal blue skies. Not familiar at all with horses, I watched the older men tighten their cinches before climbing on. I pretended to know what I was doing as I fiddled with my horse's cinch. But I was clueless.

When everyone saddled up, my saddle went sideways, dumping me on the ground and knocking the breath out of me. Thankfully, I was a football player, so I was accustomed to that. After the initial concern was over, we rode off, and I heard my uncle say, "Did you see how fast he fell off that horse?" Then I heard peals of laughter. I wasn't certain this was going to be a great day.

The two dogs took off running, scouting the edges of mature pines and occasionally stopping to sniff the air before running off again. Since we rode horses, we could cover a lot more territory and keep up with those running machines. It wasn't long before Babe, the lead dog, pointed on the edge of the pines. Reb, short for Rebel, soon locked in a point at a ninety-degree angle fifteen yards away. Hastily, we dismounted, shouldered our shotguns, and quick-stepped behind the frozen-in-place bird dogs, both of whom trembled with excitement.

"Whoa, Babe. Easy, Reb," my uncle soothingly said as we approached, me in the middle and my dad and uncle on either side. Suddenly, with an explosion of whirring wings, about twelve quail leaped out of the broom straw and fled. My Uncle Scott dropped two on the right. Dad dropped two on the left. My heart jumped into my throat. I never moved an inch. I was paralyzed by the sudden noise and action and never even pushed off the safety.

Dad shouted, "I got two."

Uncle Scott shouted, "I got two."

Then Dad, "Three by the biggest pine on the left. One by that large stump."

Scott shouted, "Two over there by that ditch. The rest are gone."

They marked the birds that got away. I didn't see any of that. All I saw was a cloud of gun smoke and feathers flying as I stood rooted to the ground. The dogs came back up with big smiles on their faces and mouths full of quail. My dad just looked at me and shook his head.

In a minute, Babe was on two of the escapees. As we tiptoed up behind her, I was ready this time. Babe's head was low to the ground, tail straight up in the air and muscles twitching. The birds jumped up lightning fast. I fired my 20-gauge quickly before the bird was two feet off the ground and unfortunately only a foot over Babe's head. The bird was denuded and completely cleaned in an explosion of feathers. The hair on Babe's head stood straight up, but she never moved an inch.

But not Uncle Scott. He screamed like a ten-year-old girl at her first horror movie. Babe was his prized, Blue Ribbon, national field trial champion bird dog, and I almost blew her brains out. He dropped to his knees, hugged the dog, and looked at me in dismay. Both he and my dad berated me in the strongest terms, telling me how not to shoot a bird dog. I was right. This was not going to be a good day.

Both Uncle Scott and my dad were close to their limit in short order. I had my one naked bird plus two others. Reb pointed in a briar patch in mid-morning. Dad walked up behind him just as two quail tried to escape. No such luck for them. Lightning fast, he dropped them both before they got twenty yards away. Feathers floated slowly to the ground. Then surprisingly, a third bird shot straight up, flew in a confused circle, and turned right toward my dad. In self-defense, Dad thrust the butt of his 12-gauge at the bird, striking it in mid-air and turning it around. As it flew directly away from him, Dad nailed it, adding more feathers to those already floating to the ground. We all whooped and hollered. What a great day after all!

Back at the truck, Uncle Scott loaded Babe and Reb into the dog box, where they immediately began to scratch for fleas and lick themselves. I pondered that for a moment and realized those two dogs had not stopped even for a second to scratch for three hours of solid hunting. I learned an important lesson that day:

A dog in the hunt doesn't know he has fleas.

By the same token, a man in pursuit of a higher and nobler goal doesn't know he has fleas either. By that, I mean he can't be bothered by lesser things. He is preoccupied with the accomplishment of a greater vision, a higher purpose. He will not be distracted by minor issues.

I have noticed in my medical practice that owners of businesses and CEOs rarely come to see me for minor illnesses. They tend to work while sick. They can't afford to take time off for a sore throat or a head cold. They don't usually show up at my office except for heart attacks and really bad diarrhea.

Hourly employees, on the other hand, love to see me for all manner of minor illnesses. Why? It offers a day off work

— often a paid day off work. And they ask me for three to four days off for a one-day illness. You can tell they don't own the company. They have fleas and have plenty of time to scratch and lick themselves.

One day, Jesus sat beside a well in Samaria, talking to a woman of ill repute. He was tired and hungry, but as He had begun to share good news with this woman, He forgot about physical needs. He pursued a higher and nobler aim: His Father's will. He was building the kingdom of God on earth. No time to scratch a physical need — only a strong desire to accomplish the will of His Heavenly Father. Indeed, He told the Pharisees that He "always did His Father's will."

Upon returning, the disciples were perplexed that He would talk to a half-breed Samaritan woman. Jesus told them He had "meat to eat that ye know not of" (John 4:32 KJV) — indicating that serving the higher purpose of the kingdom of God gave Him greater satisfaction and greater fulfillment and made Him forget about lesser things like physical hunger.

My brothers, when you and I pursue building the kingdom of God — whether it is sharing the gospel, making disciples, teaching fifth grade boys in Sunday school, feeding the hungry, building a Habitat house, or visiting the shut-ins — we don't have time to scratch fleas. In fact, a Christian man pursuing Jesus and the kingdom of God in earnest doesn't even know he has fleas. The little whiny, complaining things that bother most people? Well, he doesn't have time to stop for them because he's busy doing the Father's will. More importantly than this, the devil can't slide a temptation in edgewise on this guy because he's so preoccupied with Christian ministry that he can't be bothered with temptation. The old proverb, "An idle mind is the devil's workshop," is exactly correct. It's when you and I have too much free time on our hands that the devil sneaks in temptation. I've observed that men hard at work don't get into trouble, but they sure do on the weekends when they are off work and have free time at their disposal. I've learned over time that Christian boys and men need to stay busy at work and/or ministry to avoid falling into temptation. It keeps our minds on higher and nobler things and off the fleas.

A word of caution here. It's not just busyness that protects us, but rather it is love for the Father that protects our hearts. Did you catch what Jesus said? He said, "He who has my commandments and keeps them, he it is who loves me. ..." (John 14:21 NASB). When we love Him, we obey Him. When we obey Him, we demonstrate love for His Father as well. Both the Father and the Son will love us.

Being busy alone will not deliver us from the wiles of the evil one. However, an undying love for the Father will. Jesus withstood all temptation because He loved His Father and would not do anything to disappoint Him or reflect badly on Him. He always glorified His Father. Yielding to temptation does not demonstrate love — nor does it glorify our Heavenly Father.

The ultimate deliverance from temptation is for us to cultivate in our hearts an overwhelming love for Jesus — a love so strong that I would not do anything to disappoint Him. Additionally, I also advise developing a strong vision for fulfilling the Great Commission and for promoting God's kingdom on earth. Committing to these two things creates a pure-hearted, mission-minded Christian man in the hunt who usually doesn't know that he has fleas.

15

SOMEBODY CHECK ON THOMAS

God blessed our family with a Downs boy named Thomas. He is our ninth child, and the sweetest, kindest, gentlest little boy who ever lived. He loves and hugs everybody, and everybody loves him. We learn a lot of lessons in life from Thomas. We call him the Professor because God didn't send him here to learn, but rather to teach. He teaches our family how to serve, expecting nothing in return except big hugs. Because his motor skills are poor, Thomas requires a lot of serving. He's quite awkward with his hands and needs assistance bathing, shaving, and dressing. He consistently puts his shoes on backwards and never remembers to put on a belt.

Sadly for us and for him, he can't clean himself well when he goes to the bathroom. When we get ready to leave the house, various family members start shouting, "Somebody check Thomas." That means smell his rear end to determine if he did a good job cleaning himself — because if he didn't, we'll get five minutes down the road, and the truck will start to stink up and we'll have to lower the windows to get fresh air. Then back to the house we will go to get clean underwear for Thomas. Thankfully, no one can embarrass Thomas. He just smiles, waves his hand in front of his nose, and goes with the flow. He's the perfect Spirit-filled Christian, unless you mess with his Matchbox cars — but that's another story for another day and another book.

I'm sure your house is somewhat like our house, and Somebody really doesn't live there. When my wife calls from the kitchen for Somebody to check Thomas, Somebody is never home. Usually, Nobody is available and gladly responds, which means we leave the house with Thomas unchecked and wearing smelly drawers. My wife will say, "I thought I said for Somebody to check Thomas." We all look at each other questioningly, like "Who's she talking to?" That is crazy talk. That person doesn't even live here. My wife looks at me and gives me the stink-eye, and I explain to her once again, "Precious, Somebody doesn't live at our house. I'm pretty sure Nobody does, and I'll bet he's the one who failed to check Thomas."

Now, all you turkey hunters out there, aren't you glad that turkeys can't detect your odor the way that deer can? The "deer biologists" tell us a deer has nearly 300 million scent receptors, while the human nose has 5 million olfactory scent receptors and a dog has roughly 220 million ("Deer Senses and What They Mean for Bowhunters," Tyler Ridenour, posted on April 4, 2017, accessed website https://bowhunting360. com/2017/04/04/deer-senses-mean-bowhunters/ on August 11, 2019). [There's got to be a name for those guys. Maybe *deerologist* or *doeologist*. One of my uncles called me Bucko, which I'm sure was short for *buckologist.*]

How do they know that? That's why Mr. Big starts blowing at 150 yards away, despite our best efforts at covering up our scent. We turkey hunters wouldn't stand a chance if turkeys had extremely good vision, wariness, AND the scent capability of deer. We might as well give up before we even start.

I once sat in the woods late one morning, leaning against a large oak tree, and counted twelve hens feeding up a hill in the midst of large, open hardwoods. Twenty-four turkey eyes scoped out everything around them. They fed and scratched right up to where I sat without ever noticing me. Of course, I was covered in camouflage from head to toe and a camo head net. I froze in position, not moving an inch, and enjoyed watching as the late-morning sun illuminated their slow passage up hill. They took at least forty minutes to feed past me, and then they were gone. Not a single gobbler was in their midst.

My *behonkus* was completely numb by then. I had been hunting all morning and no doubt had strong man odor about me, but it didn't faze them a bit. If that had been several deer, they wouldn't have come within 100 yards of me sitting on the ground. They would have winded me and took off.

Surely you have had that heartbreaking experience.

Back in the early '80s, the pastor of my church asked the congregation a provocative question: "What would it be like if you gave off a strong, foul odor every time you sinned?"

We thought about that for a few moments and looked at each other wide-eyed as we contemplated the implications. Then a fellow named Don, who had lived a rough life before being saved, shouted from the back of the sanctuary, "I'd be the first one you'd smell." Knowing his background, we all started to laugh a little nervously.

Nonetheless, the question provoked serious discussion. We all wondered, "What if? What if our secret, sinful thoughts caused us to stink a little? What if our unconfessed sins caused us to emit a bad odor, and a deodorant wouldn't cover it up? What if more serious sins made us stink more than a lesser sin?" Oh, my! I bet we would be a more confessing people then, wouldn't we? I bet somebody could make a killing selling a deodorant called The Blood of Jesus or Power in the Blood Roll-On, and sell it in the parking lot of every church on Sunday morning.

Sometime later, Frank Peretti published a book, entitled *The Oath,* about a small town whose inhabitants exuded a thick, dark brown oily substance from their chest every time they sinned. Worse than that, the substance was malodorous and would seep through their clothing, so they couldn't hide the fact they were sinning. I thought to myself, How awesome would that be. My patients couldn't jerk me around anymore.

My routine, initial patient interview goes something like this:

"Sir, do you smoke?"

"No, Doctor, I don't smoke."

I type their response on my computer as the exam room begins to stink, and I notice a brown, oily stain appears on the front of his work shirt.

"What exactly do you mean by 'I don't smoke'?"

"Well, I knew I was coming to see you, so I quit two days ago."

"Oh, I see," I respond as I observe the rank substance running down the front of his shirt.

"Ma'am, welcome to our medical practice. Do you drink alcoholic beverages?"

"No, Sir, definitely not," she responds indignantly. As I start typing her response, and she twirls her hair, I notice her blouse turning brown and the room starting to turn rank. She looks down in horror, and then our eyes meet.

She stammers, "I … I mean … I haven't had a drink today. I quit drinking yesterday."

"So, that is your definition of not being a drinker? One day of not drinking?" She just shrugs and twirls her hair faster.

That's just a routine day in my office: lies, lies, and more lies.

Exuding thick, stinky oil from the chest when a person lies would be a great asset to my medical business. But wait a minute! What if my wife catches me watching a pretty lady at the mall?

"I saw you looking at that young lady."

"What lady?" I respond indignantly. I cover my chest with both hands instinctively, but the odor escapes anyway. I am royally undone. First, for indecent thoughts, and then for lying to my wife. Maybe this oily, rank exudate is not such a good idea after all. It might help my medical practice, but it could ruin my marriage. After all, it cuts both ways. Some things are better known by God alone to whom every man must give account.

♦　♦　♦　♦　♦

When I was ten years old, I lived with my mom's parents for a year while my dad was in basic and air commando training, prior to going to Vietnam. My grandmother employed a black lady named Lily Mae, who was five foot four and easily weighed 200 pounds. She was a fine Christian woman, and she and I became best of friends during that time. We would sit on Grandma's front porch while she shelled peas and snapped green beans and talk about the world's problems. She also had a son in Vietnam during that time.

As a ten-year-old boy, I became full of myself occasionally — smart-alecky and too big for my britches. When I got too mouthy, Lily Mae drew herself up to her full height, which was imposing to a scrawny ten-year-old boy, put one hand on her hip, and pointed her other index finger at me, and said, "Boy, you betta watch yo'self." Of course, I immediately began to mind my manners.

You can imagine my surprise some years later when I read Paul's admonition to "watch yourself" (Galatians 6:1). My mind returned to the image of Lily Mae with arms akimbo and finger pointing admonishing me, "Boy, you betta watch yo'self."

Brothers, if we don't watch ourselves and mind our manners, who will? Of course, you realize that your nose won't really grow like Pinocchio's every time you tell a lie — a very *nosable*, I mean, noticeable feature that would hold you accountable to telling the truth. We don't really have any rank, oily substance bubbling up from our shirts when we think indecent thoughts to keep us in line, so what's a Christian man to do? How do we walk in righteousness? How do you "watch yourself"?

Let me make a few suggestions:

Stick to the fundamentals. Remember what your high school or college coach told you. Never forget the fundamentals of your sport. In the Christian life, the fundamentals are always the same: abide in the Word, abide in prayer, fellowship with other believers, and submit to the lordship of Jesus Christ. Just as we lose ball games when we forget the fundamentals of our sport, we lose in the Christian life if we neglect these fundamentals.

By definition, a disciple is a disciplined individual. He disciplines himself to regularly pursue these fundamentals of the faith. As we do, we grow in grace and in the knowledge of our Lord Jesus Christ. We grow in sanctification or personal holiness. The Spirit takes our obedience to these fundamentals and makes us more like the Master.

Commit Scripture to memory. Psalm 119:11 says, "I have hidden your word in my heart that I might not sin against you." Many of us may not have memorized a verse of Scripture since we were in Vacation Bible School as an elementary student. That doesn't matter. "Your enemy the devil prowls around like a roaring lion looking for someone to devour" (1 Peter 5:8). We can either fight that dragon with a pen knife or with a two-foot long, double-edged sword. The more Scripture we know by heart, the more we have the mind of Christ, and the more we are able to resist the enemy of our souls.

That's why I have committed to memorizing a verse or

two of Scripture every week since I was in college. It gives me spiritual authority and spiritual protection. That's why people are forever accusing me of being a preacher when I'm just a country doctor. I know the word. Memorizing a verse a week from now until Jesus comes back will keep our noses from growing or our chests from stinking.

Find an accountability partner. "As iron sharpens iron, so one man sharpens another" (Proverbs 27:17). Christian men need each other. We are not intended to live our lives as loners or mavericks. God intends us to live in community with other Christian men, but Christian community is more than fish fries and wildlife banquets. You and I need at least one brother we can trust with our weaknesses and secrets. We all need someone who will pray for us and hold us up — someone who will ask us the hard questions in life to make sure we don't slip up and start to stink up.

Ideally, you would meet with an accountability partner weekly or every other week for prayer and to ask each other predetermined questions designed to keep both of you on the straight and narrow path.

Here is a list of suggested questions:
- Are you having a daily quiet time?
- What is your memory verse this week?
- Are you keeping your promises to your wife and kids?
- How are you doing at meeting your wife's emotional needs?

- Are you spending money without consulting your wife?
- Are you viewing anything on the television, internet, or movies that is inappropriate?
- Who have you shared the gospel with this week?
- How is your discipleship group?
- Have you lied about the answer to any of these questions?

My accountability partner asks me questions like this when we meet every other week, and then we pray for each other. Your list of questions may be different, but the main thing is to realize the power of having accountability in your life. We all get slack without someone looking over our shoulder. We all resist accountability, but accountability is nothing more than someone helping us keep our promises to God and our family. I want to be a promise keeper, and I'm pretty sure you do, too. You can help me, and I can help you. In the process, we can all walk in righteousness. As the commercial for Blue Emu says, "Works fast, and you won't stink."

Shake 'N' Fry Turkey

Rob Keck

2 cups milk
3 eggs, beaten
8 ounces breadcrumbs
8 wild turkey breast fillets (¼ in. thick, 3 in. long, 1½ in. wide)
Vegetable oil

In a medium bowl, mix milk and eggs. Place breadcrumbs in another bowl. Immerse turkey breasts in milk mixture, then in breadcrumbs; repeat process for double breading (which seals out excess grease from meat). Heat about 2 inches of oil in iron skillet. Drop turkey into oil for about 10 minutes, turning once. Remove turkey and drain on paper towels. Serve with Running Gear Gravy (made from the neck, back, giblets, legs, and thighs, which are cooked, browned, seasoned, cut up, and added to thickened turkey broth). Yield: 6 to 8 servings.

(As printed in *Wild About Turkey* by Rob Keck. Used by permission.)

16

CHOICES

For four days in a row, I hunted hard, trying to call the same gobbler across the river onto my property. He was responsive and vocal. I enjoyed the early morning rapport with this bird, plus two more joining us intermittently, but I wanted to engage him with some hot lead. I love hearing the songbirds awaken the morning. I love feeling the cool morning breezes and seeing the little flowers bloom in the springtime woods, especially the stray dogwoods or redbuds. I enjoy being all alone with God so we can talk about the beauty of His creation and so I can praise Him that He is "altogether lovely and altogether beautiful."

All of this pleases my soul, but I'm truly there to bag a big tom. When the first bird gobbles, worship and nature-loving flies out the window. I'm all business. I'm a serious turkey hunter. I don't mean to imply I'm a good turkey hunter because I'm not. I'm an avid hunter, but not always successful.

Often when I get home, my wife asks, "Did you 'catch' a turkey?"

I respond with my head hanging in shame, "No, ma'am, I did not bag a turkey today, but I heard three turkeys gobble." Hearing the big boys gobble is a triumph for me, so I smile anyway.

On this particular Saturday, I had until 8:30 a.m. to hunt. I had to leave early to attend my son's college graduation ceremony. The same bird gobbled right at 6:30 a.m. as usual and never stopped. He really liked my thirty-year-old Quaker Boy box call. He gobbled every fifteen minutes. Somewhere in the distance in front of me, another gobbler sounded off about 200 yards away on my side of the river. Twenty minutes later, he gobbled again, but this time 150 yards away. This was getting interesting!

About that time, a fog settled down over the river, including the river bottom where I was situated. I could only see about fifty of the 200 yards in front of me. Mr. Big across the Pacolet River sounded off and so did the newcomer on my side — right in front of me. Only now, he sounded one hundred yards away.

Suddenly, two hens appeared and began to feed slowly in my direction through a food plot I had planted the previous fall. I pushed off the safety and raised my shotgun. I sat in a lawn chair in a camo blind under an overhanging oak tree — a perfect spot for an ambush. The hens spied my decoy and fed even closer. The newcomer gobbled again at seventy-five yards, still invisible in the fog. My heart raced, and my hands sweated and trembled. I live for these moments!

I glanced at my watch. It read 8:30 a.m.!!! WHAT? You've got to be kidding! No way! Lord Jesus, have mercy! It can't be.

Life is not fair. My mind raced. I could pretend I didn't notice the time and show up late. After all, the program is two hours long, and my son won't get his diploma until the very end. Who cares about all the speakers? Surely, my loving and caring wife will understand.

I could hear her. "I can't believe you would be late for your son's graduation. You're late for everything. You don't care about this family. All you care about is hunting." Oh, my head hurt! Taking care of patients in the ICU was easier than this.

Choices, choices! What's a doctor to do?

The turkey gobbled again in the fog. The hens looked up. I expected him to appear any moment in a full strut. I knew if I saw him in a full strut, I would be paralyzed like Hercules seeing Medusa, so I shut my eyes, pushed on my safety, slipped out the back of my blind, and started up the hill to my house. Everyone in the house was getting dressed.

My wife asked, "Did you catch a turkey?" Looking at all the happy faces, I knew I had made the right choice.

I smiled, "No, ma'am, but I heard two birds gobble."

She nodded and said disinterestedly, "Hurry now, or you will be late."

We all have choices to make; some are minor and some are momentous, like leaving a gobbler in the woods when he is calling your name. Talk about a hard choice! Tear my heart out and stomp that sucker flat! Most folks just wouldn't understand.

Choices. Do I get a new truck or a used truck? Black or hunter green? Stock tires or wide mud-gripper tires? Gas or diesel? Or should I just keep hunting in the family minivan?

No, dude, cut the lace off your undies and get a real truck. Get a real truck! You're killing me!

Choices. What about turkey-hunting on Sunday? I've debated that one with my wife and with Jesus many times. It goes something like this. "There are fifty-two Sundays in the year, but only four or five in a turkey season. I can worship God forty-eight Sundays out of the year at church. Why can't I worship Him four Sundays in the woods, enjoying His creation? Jesus never says anything against turkey hunting, which to me means He is all for it."

But my wife has plenty to say. "I can't believe you would even suggest that. You're a deacon and a Sunday school teacher. What would they think if you missed church four Sundays in a row and then found out you had been turkey hunting?"

I replied, "The pastor is a turkey hunter. He would be proud of me that I wasn't a legalistic Pharisee like some people I know."

My wife wouldn't have any of that. She was a preacher's daughter. She had heard it all. She continued, "What kind of example would that set for your children?" (For most of these discussions we had lots of children around, including five daughters who didn't give two hoots in a holler about turkey hunting.)

I was cornered. Then she began preaching my own sermons to me. "I thought you were the one who said we should be faithful to our commitments, including faithful to the local church."

I kicked the sand with my hunting boots. "I guess that means I shouldn't go hunting this morning."

She replied emphatically, "No, sir, go back inside and put your Sunday suit on." My four girls started tittering, sort of like hens putting before they leave the scene when you make a bad call.

Truthfully, I sometimes hunt before church on Sunday morning. Then I scoot to the house, change clothes, put on my holy face, and go to church. Don't get me wrong, I don't think any God-fearing turkey hunter will lose his salvation if he hunts on Sunday morning. I just wouldn't make a habit of it. In fact, I wouldn't make a habit of doing anything on Sunday morning except for showing up to worship God with God's people.

◆　◆　◆　◆　◆

Kevin and his wife were patients of mine. They were not a perfect couple, but then again, who is? I counseled with them over several years, but they ended up divorced. He became depressed, but at the same time open to spiritual discussions. He and I began to meet at 6:30 a.m. at a local restaurant near my office once a week for about a year. During this time, he prospered spiritually. He was grateful for my time and attention, and we became tight friends.

Then two things happened in his life. First, he inherited a significant amount of both cash and land, which he was able to sell for even more cash. He became affluent overnight. Second, he reconnected to a female friend ten years younger than himself. He went from depressed to happy in a few months' time. He decided he didn't need me or Jesus anymore.

Kevin's situation reminded me of the story Jesus told of the hunt club owner who threw a big game banquet and invited all of his hunting buddies. After the hunt club was decorated and the barbecue prepared, he sent invitations to his friends. But all of them made excuses.

One friend excused himself by saying, "I have purchased a hunt club of my own, and I have to go survey the property and look for the best places for deer stands and food plots. Surely, you will understand." Another invited guest declined, saying he had inherited a tractor and an ATV from his grandfather, and he was eager to try them out. His best friend texted him saying that he had met a new girlfriend at the NRA banquet. "She's a looker, hunter, and a shooter — an unbeatable combination. You'll understand if I can't make it."

The hunt club owner fumed. He determined never again to have anything to do with his former friends. He had spent *bookoos* of money on the banquet, so he invited everybody at the local homeless shelter so the banquet hall would be full and the food wouldn't go to waste (Luke 14:16-23).

Does anybody in that parable sound like my friend Kevin? Does anybody in that parable sound like you? The Heavenly Father invites us to participate in the wedding feast of His Son, but we are sometimes too busy, too distracted, and too enamored with this world's toys. Be careful! He may not invite you more than once. When the door to the hunt club is shut, membership opportunity is closed forever. Outside is weeping, wailing, and gnashing of teeth.

What are the distractions that would keep a man from

accepting an invitation to a banquet thrown by God Himself? As I've observed my patients and friends over the course of my life, I have seen men reject God's invitation because of sexual indiscretion, lust for money and position, addiction to alcohol and drugs, over-commitment to hobbies (hunting, fishing, golf, softball, etc.), addiction to pornography, video-gaming, and gambling. You get the picture. You've seen all of these things yourself. None of these is worth being on the outside when the banquet hall is shut.

Before entering the Promised Land, Joshua challenged the Israelites, "Now fear the LORD and serve him with all faithfulness … But if serving the LORD seems undesirable to you, then choose for yourselves this day whom you will serve … But as for me and my household, we will serve the LORD" (Joshua 24:14-15).

It all boils down to choices. We make choices everyday: big ones and little ones. As her siblings leave the house, my daughter Hannah often shouts after them, "Make good choices." Perhaps we all need someone to shout that after us when we leave the house every day. "Make good choices."

17

COMMUNICATION

My friend Harold picked me up before daylight, and we drove in near silence to our hunt club on Jerusalem Church Road below Pacolet, South Carolina. The conversation was brief and to the point.

"Looks like a good day to hunt," I remarked.

"Uh-huh."

"They ought to be gobbling," I speculated.

"I reckon."

Harold was a big talker in the early morning. We made the thirty-five-minute trip in silence, contemplating the possibilities. We were hopeful, as are all hunters and fishermen before they enter the woods or go onto the water.

We approached the locked gate of our hunt club as the eastern sky brightened. After passing through the gate, we parked the truck one-quarter mile farther down a rutted clay road. Slipping out of the truck quietly, we donned our turkey vests and loaded our shotguns. We could see each other's breath in the early morning cold.

Harold nodded to the roadbed and said, "I'll go down the hill."

I looked to the right past an old abandoned homesite. "Okay. I'll go right. See you back at 10 a.m."

"Bag a big one," Harold said over his shoulder as he disappeared into the semi-darkness.

I heard two birds gobble close by that morning and multiple other birds in the distance — too far to pursue. The close-up birds were not interested in me.

I met Harold back at the truck at 10 a.m., invigorated by the long walk through the deep woods — observing dogwoods and red and lavender redbuds blooming and bright yellow daffodils at the old home site. Hearing turkeys gobble in the wild always made me smile. (Do you know how few people have heard a wild turkey gobble in the deep woods? I'm not talking about on television or at a petting zoo, but in the wild woods where turkey and deer roam free.) The exercise is good for me. Experiencing nature is a gift from God. Connecting with the Maker of the heavens and the earth is especially easy in the quiet of the deep woods where little birds continually sing His praise and the rising sun shows His majesty and glory.

Harold asked, "Hear anything?"

"Yeah, a couple."

"See anything?"

"Nah. You?"

"Nuthin'. Let's go."

We loaded our gear in the truck and retraced our steps in near silence to my house, contemplating the morning's experience.

I asked, "Do you think they are all still henned up?"

"Yeah, I do. Still early in the season."

Back at my house, Harold said, "Maybe next week it will be better."

"Yeah, call me Thursday, and we'll line up our schedules."

As Harold drove off, I walked into the back door of our house where my wife was sitting at the kitchen counter. In an offhand remark, I said, "That Harold, he sure is a great guy. He's got to be one of my best friends."

My wife looked at me and said, "I'm sure he is. What did y'all talk about?"

My mind went blank. What did we talk about? What kind of question was that? My mind raced back over the morning. Again, what did we talk about? I looked at my wife and responded, "Oh, just stuff," and brushed on past.

Now, I would like for you to compare that heart-warming, man-bonding experience with what happened to me the next weekend.

My wife and one of her friends needed to go to Atlanta for some reason and asked me to drive them. I don't know what came over me, but I decided I needed time to think about some things. So, I agreed — three hours there and three hours back.

I got behind the wheel with them in the backseat and settled in for a leisurely three-hour drive with plenty of time to relax and think. Wrong, Bucko! Those two women talked back and forth so fast it was like — like a machine gun! I couldn't even follow the conversation. They talked over the top of one another, laughing and cackling like old boss hens.

Before fifteen minutes had elapsed, my rational mind told me to admit defeat, turn around, and go home. However, my pride would not allow that. I had made a commitment. Besides, I knew my wife would jerk a knot in my head if I came close to implying she talked too much. (She is shaking her head even now while typing this for me. Not sure she should.)

By the time we were halfway to Atlanta, I felt like screaming. I couldn't tell if my brain was going to shrink or explode. I could no longer make logical decisions, and I was losing touch with reality. I'm pretty sure I was starting to hallucinate. I saw a psychiatric hospital beside the interstate, and I considered checking myself in. It might have been a lack of oxygen in the truck because I'm pretty sure they used it all up, except when they stopped to tell me to slow down or watch out for that car — an all too frequent occurrence. Just remembering that six hours of automatic fire talk makes me a nervous jerk.

You understand men are different than women. When I drive somewhere with my daughters, they talk to me — or, should I say, they talk and I listen. When I drive somewhere with my sons, we experience blessed silence. It's a guy thing.

◆   ◆   ◆   ◆   ◆

Failure to communicate is common in every area of life and can lead to comical or disastrous consequences. Consider Buck and Beulah Mae — patients of mine who had serious communication issues.

I entered Exam Room #1 and found Beulah Mae sitting in

the chair with her eyes red and puffy from weeping. Her face was in her hands, and she wouldn't look up. Buck leaned against the exam table with a pack of Marlboros in his shirt pocket and a plastic straw in his teeth. He stared at his wife with a look of puzzlement on his face.

"What can I do for you guys today?" I queried.

Buck shrugged as if he did not know why they were in my office. He probably was clueless. Beulah Mae looked up at me with red-rimmed eyes and snubbed, "Dr. Jackson, he won't talk to me."

Buck immediately took the defensive with "Whaddya mean? I talk to you all the time."

With fire in her eyes, she exploded with sarcasm, "'What's for supper' and 'are you going to bed with me' are not great conversation. Food and sex are all he ever thinks or talks about."

"That's not true. I talk to you about my bird dogs all the time."

"Oh, yeah. He tells me about his prize-winning bird dogs. He comes home from work and goes straight out to the dog lot. He doesn't help with cleaning up after supper or putting the kids to bed. He loves those dogs more than me or the kids. Then he goes to bed at night smelling like diesel fuel, axle grease, and dog hair. He won't bathe until morning. He wants me to be intimate with him smelling like that. He's crazy. He gets grease on me and my bed sheets. He's disgusting."

Buck got fired up then. "Now looka here, little lady. I'm proud of what I do. That fuel oil smell and axle grease is what pays the bills around our home. I don't run around on you like your first husband. I quit smoking weed like you asked me to. I don't drink. Sure, I smoke a little baca, but that ain't nothing compared to your sorry coke-head ex-husband."

Beulah Mae opened her mouth and shut it about three times. She didn't know what to say next. I figured I better intervene before physical violence broke out. I looked at Buck and asked, "Do you know the way to a man's heart?"

He smiled proudly. "Sure do. I heard my mama say it a thousand times: through his stomach. Now my wife is a fine cook. I've gained twenty pounds in the two years we've been married. If I'm not careful, I'll be as big as my daddy."

"All right. Do you know the way to a woman's heart?"

He stared at me blankly for a moment. Then he lifted his big arms, tapped his biceps, and smiled. "These guns. They'll do it."

I thought Beulah Mae was going to throw up. I shook my head swiftly and made the sound of a buzzer as on a game show when you give the wrong reply. "No, sir, wrong answer. The way to a woman's heart is through the kitchen."

He tipped his head and stared at me sideways through squinty eyes.

"If you want to win your wife's heart, you have to start in the kitchen. All romance starts in the kitchen with cleaning up the dirty dishes, washing the pots and pans, and putting away the leftovers. When you serve your wife in that way, you will win her affection. Better than that, if you bathe the kids, put on their PJs, and put them to bed, you will become her superhero. She will then be overcome with romance, but

ONLY if you bathe before bedtime."

He stared again and then responded, "But, but, Doc, that's squaw work."

It was my turn to stare blankly. "Excuse me?"

"Brave Indian warriors don't wash dishes or put kids to bed."

"Oh, I see. That's beneath your dignity."

"Not necessarily. It's just I bring home the bacon. I cut the grass, pull the weeds, take care of the dogs. That's man work. Taking care of the house, that's squaw work. I don't do squaw work."

"I understand, and that's why you don't get any loving or respect either."

His eyes glazed over, and he stared at me once again.

"Buck, let me explain something to you. In the Bible, Jesus said, 'I didn't come to be served but to serve and to give my life a ransom for many.' Jesus gave Himself sacrificially on our behalf to purchase our redemption. He came as a servant among men. More than that, we men are challenged to love our wives as 'Christ loved the church and gave himself for her' (Ephesians 5:25).

"Genuine romance in your marriage starts with you being a servant to your wife. Forget the artificial division of labor; start serving your wife in the kitchen and putting the kids to bed on top of everything else you do. This requires sacrifice. Beulah Mae needs to know she and the kids are more important than anything else in your life. Sell the dogs if you must. Do whatever it takes to convince her she is number one in your life. The romantic love will follow, but, trust me, it begins in the kitchen with you serving her and the children sacrificially.

Does this make sense to you?"

Beulah Mae beamed. I spoke the truth she had tried to tell him for two years. Buck looked at the floor and twirled his straw.

"Yeah, it makes perfect sense, Doc. You sound just like my grandpa. You know he's a preacher. I just don't know if I can do it. I just don't know if it's in me." Then he looked at me with a look of desperation on his face.

"Buck, you want to know a hard truth?"

He responded warily, "Sure."

"You can't … and neither can I. Only the spirit of God can enable us to live and love like Jesus. It requires the grace of God in our lives to love our wives the way Jesus loved the church. You told me once before that you had been born again and were confident of your salvation. Is that still true?"

He nodded confidently.

"Then you have everything you need to partake of the divine nature (2 Peter 1:3) and to love your wife as you should. I would start by confessing that you haven't been doing things well and make a commitment that, by God's grace, you are going to do better."

Again, he nodded ever so slowly. And Beulah Mae smiled.

"Oh, and don't forget to shower before bedtime. Just saying."

The previous incident is a true story. The names have been changed, of course, to protect the innocent or the guilty, as the case may be.

Buck has two primary issues that afflict many of my male patients: poor communication skills and lack of a servant's heart. We address the remedy for the lack of a servant's heart in the illustration above. Let's discuss communication skills a bit more.

Men are good at superficial listening. We don't pay close attention to our wives or children when they talk to us. We continue to read our hunting magazines, look at our phones, or watch the football game while they try to communicate with us. We mumble something unintelligible at appropriate intervals feigning interest. My brothers, any pig can grunt.

Put down your phone. Turn off the television. Look your wife in the eyes and give her your undivided attention. She is the love of your life and the queen of your heart. Treat her respectfully as if that were true. Try repeating back to her what she says so she knows you are listening and understanding. Try the following words: "So what I hear you saying is …" She'll love you for being her best friend who really talks to her, listens to her, and understands her. Do not allow some other lady friend to fill that role in her life. You should be her best friend who truly listens and understands.

The next level of communication is easy for us guys because it requires sharing only what we think — our opinion. We men love to share our opinion. We become instant experts on all manner of things about which we know practically nothing. Our children can fondly say about us, "Dad may not always be right, but he rarely lacks confidence."

Sharing the facts that you know and the opinions that you hold don't require a great deal of transparency or intimacy. It is a level of communication we men can share with a good many people in our circle of influence. We enjoy sharing information and opinions because it makes us look smart or perhaps like a "know it all" to our kids.

It starts to get a little tricky and sticky at the next level because here we must share our emotions. At this level, we share how we feel. Instead of saying, "I'll tell you what I think about that," we must admit, "Well, that breaks my heart" or "That really makes me mad." This is the beginning of true communication. Our womenfolk are good at this, but we men are like wooden statues. It is not that we don't have emotions; we're just not good at sharing them. We think it conveys weakness. "There is no crying in baseball" is a notion that is true in all of life for many of us. Letting our wives or friends know how we really feel is threatening.

Why is that? Men fear rejection. They may not like the real us if we reveal the emotional part of us. That's why the circle of people to whom we reveal our emotions is limited. This circle must include trusted confidantes who understand confidentiality and who will love us regardless of our revealed emotions. At this level, we share our hopes, dreams, fears, disappointments, joys, sorrows, failures, desires, stresses, sources of fulfillment, and discouragements. Our wives then begin to understand who we are and become our best friends — not just household companions who cook, clean, wash our clothes, and birth our children.

The deepest level of communication is the most difficult for men and women. This transcends emotional communication and becomes transparent communication, which involves sharing our hearts. This requires complete emotional and personal truthfulness.

In the garden, Adam and Eve "were both naked, and they felt no shame" (Genesis 2:25). They were totally exposed and fully accepted until sin entered. Then, they covered their nakedness and hid from God. We do the same thing. Because of our sinfulness, we hide from God and from each other. This makes transparency hard, but not impossible. Who likes to be naked and exposed? This takes courage and a lot of genuine love. This kind of communication will occur primarily between spouses.

However, there are a few things that transparency is not. Transparency is not psychological nakedness where we share everything about ourselves with everyone. That would be verbal streaking! Nor is transparency verbal impulsiveness, which is saying what we feel when we feel like saying it. That would be like living next to an active volcano with frequent eruptions. Transparency does mean sharing our feelings and emotions — our hearts — with someone who is committed to us. It means being vulnerable with that one trusted individual.

I know what you guys are thinking. "Doc, I'm a whole lot like you and Harold. I consider myself the strong silent type. My wife talks and I listen. I got off the train at the level of sharing my opinion. I'd rather have a colonoscopy without anesthesia than open wide my heart like you're talking about."

Let me explain what Buck did not understand. There are benefits to being transparent with your spouse. First, we can only understand as much of ourselves as we are able to communicate to another person — our spouse. This takes hard work and a lot of introspection, but leads to self-understanding and emotional maturity. That means we must practice explaining to our spouse how we feel. Second, transparency communicates love to our spouse more than gifts. Transparency says, "I need you and I trust you." Sharing at this level is an act of love. I admit it is a bit risky, but real love is risky business. Don't forget the Scripture says, "There is no fear in love. But perfect love drives out fear" (1 John 4:18).

Here's the kicker. Satan's goal for our marriages is isolation and divorce. God's goal is unity, oneness, and an accurate portrayal of that mystical union between Jesus and His bride, the Church. When we achieve transparency with our spouse, it defeats isolation and leads to oneness between us and our spouse. Although we all may not be able to verbalize it, on some level we intuitively know that poor communication and poor relationships go hand-in-hand and inevitably lead to isolation.

The older I get, the more comfortable I am being like Robert and Harold. I talk less and share my emotions less frequently. I still enjoy sharing my opinions. I just can't help myself with that. However, I don't want to be like Buck who has serious marital issues. I've made a commitment to practice sharing my emotions, hurts, dreams, weaknesses, triumphs, and goals with my lovely bride. I figured out awhile back that my intimacy with God is somehow proportional to my level of transparency with my mate. If I improve one, somehow I improve the other. It cuts both ways. Just don't ask me to explain it.

All of you guys are aware that your wife has a girlfriend or two with whom she talks, talks, talks. They are good friends, and they share their emotions with one another. If you are not careful, your wife will end up getting her emotional needs met by a lady friend and not by you. She will gradually shift her allegiance and loyalty from you to her friends who truly listen to her and understand her (God forbid that the friend should be another man who listens and begins to meet her emotional needs).

My brother, I have told you already that Scripture tells us in 1 Peter 3:7 to live with our wives in a considerate, understanding way, which includes considering how to be a good listener, sharing your emotions, being transparent, and allowing her to see into your heart. This allows you to become her very best friend who actually talks to her (remember Beulah Mae's complaint with Buck was that he never talked to her) and understands her.

Now, I know this strikes fear into your heart. You would rather be shot in the rear end with rat shot from twenty yards than even think about attempting all of this! I'm here to tell you that the investment in communication with your spouse will net for you dividends in your relationship that you would never anticipate. Your spiritual connection will improve. Intimacy will improve. Understanding will improve. Friendship will improve. Next thing you know, she'll be telling her friends, "You know — that husband of mine — he's really a great guy; he's got to be my best friend."

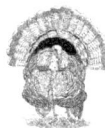

(Photo by Shoeib Abolhassani, Unsplash.com)

18

THE WORSHIPPING WOODSMAN

God gave me this chapter recently while sitting in a deer stand trying to make my mind focus on worshipping Him, which can be difficult due to distractions. My heart was in it because of the beauty of the woods, but squirrels running, acorns falling, and crows calling distracted my mind. You know what I mean!

I'm currently sitting in a ground blind, deer hunting with my twenty-six-year-old special needs son JR, who is hoping to bag his first deer with a crossbow. I am excited for him, and, boy, is he pumped! He asks me every ten minutes in a hoarse whisper, "Dad, where the deer?"

I whisper back, "I don't know."

He doesn't hear well, so he asks me again, "Dad, where the deer?"

I lean over and speak into his hearing aid, "I don't know" for the tenth time.

"Oh, ok." Ten minutes later, he asks, "Dad, when the deer coming?" He constantly asks deep theological questions like

"Pastor Hank hunt today? Why acorns fall? Why sky blue? Where the deer?"

My stock answers usually suffice: "I don't know," or "That's the way God made it." I think I prefer his Downs brother, who is nonverbal! At least JR can't hear the squirrels and the acorns falling, or he would be constantly asking, "Is that a deer?"

When I was in medical school, I worked for three months in a missionary hospital in the Middle East in the Gaza Strip, courtesy of the Southern Baptist International Mission Board. It was a great experience since I worked side-by-side in the medical clinic with the internist, Dr. Lynne Abney, and in the OR with the surgeon, Dr. Dean Fitzgerald. I also took call in the ER at night. This boosted my confidence and competence.

One day when riding my bicycle to the clinic, I saw a group of Middle Eastern youth practicing with a sling, hurling stones at a target. I stopped to watch, fascinated by their accuracy and by the explosive impact of their projectiles. The sling was composed of two leather strips about two and a half feet long with a pouch in the middle into which they placed a stone three-to-five inches in diameter that weighed one-to-two pounds. Their target was a large rock set on a stone wall in an empty lot in Gaza City. They had a pile of carefully selected round sling stones. (The Middle East is absolutely covered with stones. Homes are made with stone, and the same homes and pastures are surrounded by stone walls built with stones removed from the pastures.)

The hurler then swung the stone around his head with increasing velocity, making a low-pitched humming sound both thrilling and fearful — thrilling if you are the assailant and fearful if you are the prey and don't know exactly where the assailant is located but can hear that awful sound. When the hurler achieved the right velocity, he released his stone with amazing accuracy. The stone target and the projectile exploded into hundreds of fragments to the immense delight of the teenage boys.

I admit I was impressed and delighted. It reminded me of the Scripture describing the men of Benjamin who could throw a stone at a hair and never miss (Judges 20:16). For some reason, I thought David killed Goliath with a smooth stone one-to-two inches in size that weighed an ounce or two. Those Middle Eastern youth disabused me of my vain imagining. I have a round sling stone weighing about two pounds from the Middle East that I keep on my dresser. It is quite impressive. While holding it in my hand, I realize how devastating it could be.

Before David was the king of Israel who lived in a palace, he was an outdoorsman, a shepherd, a hunter, and a warrior. He spent long hours outdoors in the Middle Eastern heat by day and in the cold by night, tending and guarding his sheep. He knew the weather and the seasons. He understood the habits of his sheep and their predators. He was also a hunter. He once told King Saul that when a bear or a lion took one of his sheep that he tracked them and killed them (1 Samuel 17:34-37). He didn't have a high-powered rifle or a compound bow. He probably had a spear and a knife.

How would you like to single-handedly track a bear or a lion with just a spear? We could start a new reality TV show Ultimate Challenge and invite people to track and kill a lion or bear with just a spear. We could video the whole thing. You know we would get plenty of brave and foolish volunteers. The only problem is the liability would probably be too great, because the lion and the bear might win too often. Oh, well, another great idea down the drain!

David was a fearless and superlative hunter. He was an equally fearless leader of men in battle. David and his mighty men conquered all the Middle East from the Mediterranean to the Euphrates River. The songwriter of Israel was also a genuine worshiper of God and a man after God's own heart. His appreciation of the outdoors shines through in his Psalms. Psalm 19:1-6 says:

> *The heavens declare the glory of God; the skies proclaim the work of his hands. Day after day they pour forth speech; night after night they display knowledge. There is no speech or language where their voice is not heard. Their voice goes out into all the earth, their words to the ends of the world. In the heavens he has pitched a tent for the sun, which is like a bridegroom coming forth from his pavilion, like a champion rejoicing to run his course. It rises at one end of the heavens and makes its circuit to the other; nothing is hidden from its heat.*

David sat on a hillside all alone often enough to observe the stars in the night sky and the sun in its march across the morning sky "like a champion rejoicing to run his course" (Psalm 19:5b). Silent, without speech, yet declaring the glory of God. You've done that. I've done that. Why didn't we think up those verses? David did it for us and gave it to us as a gift from God — one worshiping outdoorsman to another.

All of us fancy ourselves to be outdoorsmen, hunters, and a warrior type like David. We even think we are the king of our castle (when our wives allow it), but what about the worship part? Are we as good about worshiping God as David was?

When I sit in the deep woods, my heart is often filled to bursting with the overwhelming joy of experiencing the deep blue sky, the majestic oaks, the wind whispering in the tall pines, and the birds singing the praise of God Almighty. My soul fills with exaltation at the privilege of seeing a deer tiptoe silently through deep fallen leaves or hearing tom turkey gobble in the distance or seeing a mama bobcat with her three kittens walking under my stand, thinking she is unnoticed.

"From the rising of the sun to the place where it sets, the name of the Lord is to be praised" (Psalm 113:3).

I try to give expression to this joy in my heart when I'm sitting in a deer stand or under over-hanging limbs calling turkeys, but I have a problem. One, I get terribly distracted, and, two, I can't think of exactly what to say. I solved the second problem years ago by writing on a five-by-seven index card nine attributes of God with part of a Scripture verse beside it that described that attribute.

For example, holiness: "Holy, holy, holy is the Lord Almighty. The whole earth is full of his glory" (Isaiah 6:3).

Lovingkindness: "Know therefore that the LORD your God, He is God, the faithful God, who keeps His covenant and His lovingkindness to a thousandth generation with those who love Him and keep His commandments" (Deuteronomy 7:9 NASB).

You get the picture. I carried these cards in my hunting gear and pulled them out to look at and memorize when the joy of being outdoors overcame me. I prayed through those verses, praising God for those attributes. Eventually, I memorized all those verses and added more. Now, I have a pretty good vocabulary of praise verses.

Dealing with distractions is more difficult. Every little squirrel that runs down a tree, and every branch that breaks sounds like a deer or turkey to me. I immediately go on high alert. Whatever worshipful attitude I might have had goes out the camo blind. I must discipline myself to come back to worshipping God after my heart rate slows down, and I begin to breath normally again.

Why do I do this? Because God is worthy of my soul's best songs. He made me from the dust of the earth and breathed into me the breath of life. He gave me eyes that see, ears that hear, and a strong physical body that can work and hunt. If that were not enough, He loved me enough to redeem me from hell and the grave.

♦ ♦ ♦ ♦ ♦

Praise Him! Praise Him!
Jesus, our blessed Redeemer!
Sing, O earth,
His wonderful love proclaim
Hail Him! Hail Him!
Highest archangels in glory;
Strength and honor
Give to His holy name!
("Praise Him! Praise Him!" by Fanny J. Crosby)

Go bag a big one. While you're out there, remember to give God the glory! And thanks for letting me share a few ideas from the country doctor's rusty, dusty scrapbook. God bless!

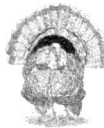

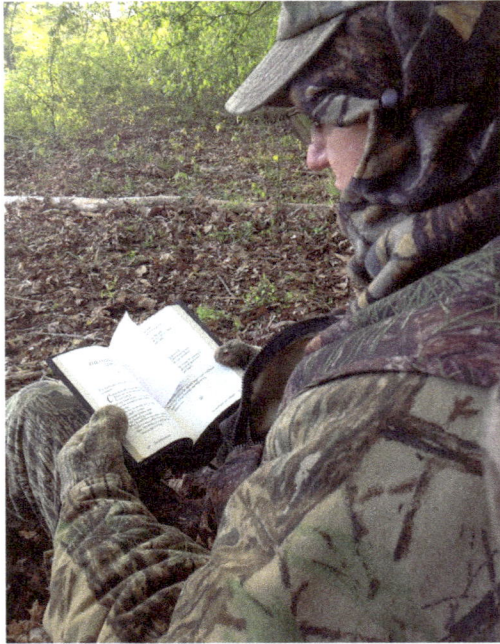

Reading, pondering, and worshipping my Creator, my Lord, and my Savior.

(Feel free to clip, copy and share these pages)

Attributes of God (NASB)

Holiness —

"Holy, holy, holy is the LORD of hosts,
The whole earth is full of His glory" (Isaiah 6:3).

Lovingkindness —

"But Thou, O Lord, art a God merciful and gracious,
Slow to anger and abundant in lovingkindness and
truth" (Psalm 86:15).

Merciful —

"The LORD is gracious and merciful;
Slow to anger and great in lovingkindness"
(Psalm 145:8).

Forgiving —

"As far as the east is from the west,
So far has He removed our transgressions from us"
(Psalm 103:12).

Just —

"The Rock! His work is perfect,
For all His ways are just;
A God of faithfulness and without injustice,
Righteous and upright is He" (Deuteronomy 32:4).

Eternal —

> "Now to the King eternal, immortal, invisible,
> the only God, be honor and glory forever and ever.
> Amen" (1 Timothy 1:17).

Almighty — "And I heard, as it were, the voice of
> a great multitude and as the sound of many waters
> and as the sound of mighty peals of thunder,
> saying, 'Hallelujah! For the Lord our God,
> the Almighty, reigns'" (Revelation 19:6).

Names of Jesus (NASB)

Good Shepherd —
> "I am the good shepherd;the good shepherd lays down his life for the sheep" (John 10:11).

The Resurrection and the Life —
> "I am the resurrection and the life; he who believes in Me shall live even if he dies" (John 11:25).

The Way, the Truth, and the Life —
> "I am the way, and the truth, and the life; no one comes to the Father, but through me" (John 14:6).

The Bread of Life —
> "I am the bread of life; he who comes to Me shall not hunger, and he who believes in Me shall never thirst" (John 6:35).

The Light of the World —
> "I am the light of the world; he who follows Me shall not walk in the darkness, but shall have the light of life" (John 8:12).

Bright Morning Star —
> "I am the root and the offspring of David, the bright, morning star" (Revelation 22:16b).

King of Kings and Lord of Lords —

"And on His robe and on His thigh He has a name
written, 'KING OF KINGS, AND LORD OF LORDS'"
(Revelation 19:16).

Lamb of God —

"The next day he saw Jesus coming to him, and said,
'Behold, the Lamb of God who takes away the sin of
the world'" (John 1:29).

Great Physician —

"Go and report to John what you hear and see: the
blind receive sight and the lame walk, the lepers are
cleansed and the deaf hear, and the dead are raised
up, and the poor have the gospel preached to them"
(Matthew 11:4-5).

Immanuel —

"'Behold, the virgin shall be with child, and shall bear
a son, and they shall call His name 'Immanuel,' which
translated means, 'God with us'" (Matthew 1:23).

Prince of Peace —

"For a child will be born to us, a son will be given to us;
And the government will rest on His shoulders; And
His name will be called Wonderful Counselor, Mighty
God, Eternal Father, Prince of Peace" (Isaiah 9:6).

A Final Note

I have been a loyal supporter of National Wild Turkey Federation for over 30 years because of their dedication to hunter education, conservation, and development of turkey populations across the United States. My financial support of local NWTF banquets contributes to the overall success of their goals and objectives both locally and nationally. When I see an abundance of wild turkeys in a pasture in the distance, I am always thankful for their efforts. I encourage my readers to learn about NWTF, to become a member, and a to be a loyal financial supporter. Without organizations like NWTF, our opportunity to hunt could very easily disappear in years to come.

— *Dr. Robert E. Jackson Jr.*

About the NWTF

When the National Wild Turkey Federation was founded in 1973, there were about 1.3 million wild turkeys in North America. After decades of dedicated work, that number hit a historic high of almost 7 million turkeys. The foundation of our success? Standing behind science-based conservation and hunters' rights.

Thanks to the tremendous efforts of our dedicated volunteers, professional staff and committed partners, we have had many successes that advanced our mission. Together, we have facilitated the investment of nearly half a billion dollars in wildlife conservation and the preservation of North America's hunting heritage. Our returns have included improving more than 20 million acres of wildlife habitat and introducing 100,000 people to the outdoors each year.

The mission of the National Wild Turkey Federation is no less urgent today than when it was founded in 1973. What we do in the coming decades will be instrumental in not only enhancing wild turkey populations but also in the continuation of hunting and quality wildlife habitat for countless species.

We're losing 6,000 acres of habitat every day. Hunters fund conservation but now we're at the point where less than 10 percent of the American population hunts, so the funding source is going away. We know we can't solve this alone. It's bigger than one organization. The NWTF is leading a collaborative effort to solve the problem with the "Save the Habitat. Save the Hunt" initiative, and our contribution is our dynamic volunteer base.

Since 1985, NWTF volunteers and partners raised and spent nearly half a billion dollars toward our mission of conserving wildlife habitat and preserving our hunting heritage.

(Used by permission of National Wild Turkey Federation)

National Wild Turkey Federation
770 Augusta Road
Edgefield, South Carolina 29824
Phone: 803.637.3106 | Fax: 803.637.0034 | Webpage: www.nwtf.org

Dr. Jackson and his wife, Carlotta, their nine children, four sons-in-law, one daughter-in-law, and eight grandchildren (two more grandchildren have been added).

The Jacksons can be contacted for questions or for speaking engagements via their Facebook and website pages, under the name "Jackson Family Ministry." Also, you can hear them speak on a wide range of topics, but always through the lens of a biblical worldview, on their podcast entitled "More Than Medicine."

OTHER BOOKS BY DR. JACKSON

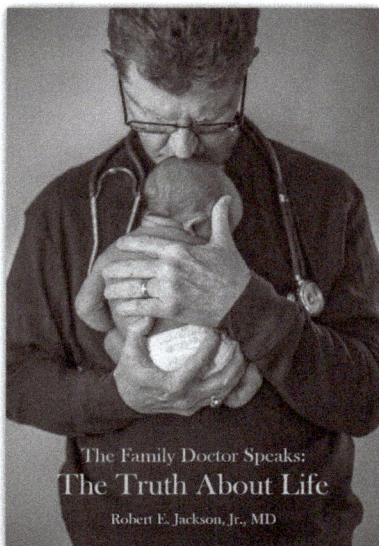

*The Family Doctor Speaks:
The Truth About Life*
(available at Amazon.com
and BarnesandNoble.com)

*The Family Doctor Speaks:
The Truth About
Seed Planting*
(available at
CourierPublishing.com,
Amazon.com, and
BarnesandNoble.com)

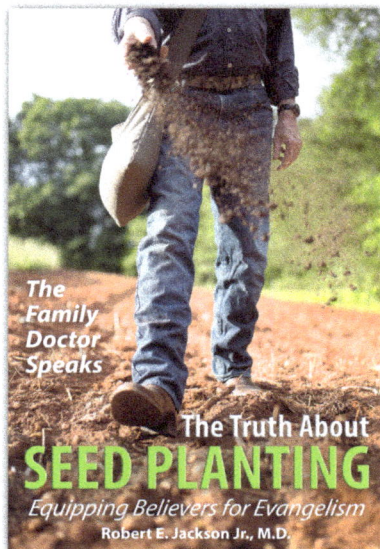